Easy
Appliqué Samplers

20 Designs to Mix and Match

Mimi Dietrich

Martingale®
& COMPANY

DEDICATION

To all of my students—you inspire me!

ACKNOWLEDGMENTS

EACH PROJECT STARTS with an idea and comes to life with the help of many wonderful people.

My thanks to Karen Soltys, who believed in my ideas, and to Mary Green and the editorial staff at Martingale, who create magic with quilt ideas.

Many thanks to the following friends and "graduate" students who quilted and appliquéd using a wide variety of techniques to make the appliqué samplers come alive!

Anita Askins, Barbara Bennett, Robin Blackburn, Barbara Blue, Julie Bradley, Pamela Budesheim, Norma Campbell, Ann Christy, Genie Corbin, Joan Costello, Mary Ellen DeMaio, Annette Dietrich, Angie Dukehart, Eleanor Eckman, Nancy Egan, Sherri Eisenstein, Brenda Finnegan, Patsy Glynn, Laurie Gregg, Vera Hall, Jean Harmon, Diana Harper, Pat Hersl, Lynn Irwin, Barbara Kopf, Kelly Kout, Barbara Laskowski, Elaine Loughlin, Bonnie Maneer, Dori Mayer, Debra McCarriar, Marylou McDonald, Barbara McMahon, Polly Mello, Betty Morton, Clara Murphy, Linda Newsom, Helen Quane, Barbara Rasch, Robbyn Robinson, Libbie Rollman, Dot Savage, Joan Schachnuk, Vivian Schaefer, Linda Schiffer, Sandy Schlossberg, Ruth Scott, Penny Seymore, Kathy Siuta, Patty Stenpeck, Mary Stewart, Millie Tracey, Helen Watkins, Connie Waxter, Alice White, Kay Worley

CREDITS

President: *Nancy J. Martin*
CEO: *Daniel J. Martin*
Publisher: *Jane Hamada*
Editorial Director: *Mary V. Green*
Managing Editor: *Tina Cook*
Technical Editor: *Cyndi Hershey*
Copy Editor: *Sheila Chapman Ryan*
Design Director: *Stan Green*
Illustrators: *Brian Metz and Laurel Strand*
Cover Designer: *Stan Green*
Text Designer: *Trina Craig*
Photographer: *Brent Kane*

Easy Appliqué Samplers:
20 Designs to Mix and Match
© 2005 by Mimi Dietrich

MISSION STATEMENT

Dedicated to providing quality products and service to inspire creativity.

That Patchwork Place® is an imprint of Martingale & Company®.

Martingale & Company
20205 144th Avenue NE
Woodinville, WA 98072-8478 USA
www.martingale-pub.com

Printed in China
10 09 08 07 06 05   8 7 6 5 4 3 2 1

Library of Congress Cataloging-in-Publication Data
Dietrich, Mimi.
    Easy appliqué samplers : 20 Designs to Mix and Match / Mimi Dietrich.
        p. cm.
    Includes bibliographical references and index.
    ISBN 1-56477-562-3 (alk. paper)
    1. Appliqué—Patterns. 2. Quilting—Patterns. I. Title.
    TT779.D5425 2005
    746.44'5041—dc22
                                           2004024673

Contents

Introduction

I LOVE APPLIQUÉ! There's something magical about creating designs with colorful fabrics and appliqué stitches. It's exciting to choose fabrics that are perfect for the appliquéd shapes and watch the designs come alive. It's like painting pictures with fabric. My favorite quilts are always the appliquéd ones.

In the past, young girls practiced their needlework by stitching samplers. These antique needlework designs inspired the projects in this book. Appliqué samplers include some of the same elements as needlework samplers—a central picture, letters, and a border. They also provide opportunities for you to learn different appliqué techniques. You can try traditional appliqué, needle-turn techniques, or freezer-paper techniques, and then add a touch of dimensional appliqué or embroidery. You can mix hand appliqué with machine appliqué. It's fun to learn new techniques on small projects, and experimenting helps you decide which methods you like best.

The definition of the word appliqué is "to apply." Appliqué pieces are cut from selected fabrics and sewn on top of a background fabric to create beautiful designs with curves, flowers, and realistic shapes. Traditional appliqué is done by hand, but you can also create beautiful appliqué with your sewing machine. I love relaxing in my favorite chair with hand appliqué, but when I need a fast project I turn to my machine. The most wonderful thing about appliqué is that there are so many different ways to do it.

Hand appliqué is very portable. You can prepare your project pieces, organize them in small plastic bags, and take them wherever you go. You can stitch during a Little League game, a visit to the doctor, or while sitting on a friend's porch on a fresh spring day. Invite a few friends over and appliqué while you visit.

Machine appliqué is a faster method. You can prepare the pieces while you travel or visit with a friend, but you need a sewing machine to attach the pieces to the background fabric. Machine stitches can even make your appliqués look like they are stitched by hand. For a superfast project, simply fuse the appliqués to the background. Machine appliqué is a great method for sewing presents or just getting things done quickly.

I use the techniques in this book to teach students successful appliqué skills. As you learn more about appliqué, you will discover many other techniques and tricks to make it easier and more fun. Listen to other stitchers and teachers. Some techniques work better for different people and in different situations. Try them all; then use the ones you like the best.

Each appliqué sampler includes suggested appliqué techniques, but you can use your favorite methods for any of them. All of the quilts in this book can be stitched using hand or machine techniques. I hope you enjoy sampling these designs!

Mimi

Appliqué Terms

HERE ARE SOME common appliqué terms you may find helpful.

Appliqué: A method of sewing pieces of fabric on top of a larger background fabric piece to create a design.

Appliqué stitch: A small, nearly invisible stitch used to attach appliqué fabric to the background fabric.

Background fabric: A large piece of fabric to which appliqué shapes are stitched.

Basting: Temporarily holding fabric in place by stitching, pinning, or gluing.

Bias: A diagonal line that runs at a 45° angle to the threads in the fabric. Fabric has the greatest amount of stretch on the bias.

Freezer-paper appliqué: A method of preparing appliqué shapes using templates cut from freezer paper.

Fusible appliqué: A method of using a fusible-web product and an iron to fuse appliqué pieces to the background fabric.

Fussy cutting: Cutting an appliqué piece from a specific area of a fabric design, such as leaves or flowers.

Glue basting: Using a dab of glue stick to temporarily hold fabric in place.

Hand appliqué: Stitching the appliqués to the background fabric using hand-sewing techniques.

Hand basting: Using a hand-sewing needle, thread, and running stitches to temporarily hold fabric in place.

Layered appliqué: A design with appliqués that overlap other appliquéd pieces.

Machine appliqué: Using a sewing machine to sew appliqués to the background fabric. You can use a straight, zigzag, or decorative machine stitch.

Needle-turn appliqué: A method of turning the seam allowance of the appliqué pieces under as you sew them to the background fabric.

Pattern overlay: The appliqué pattern is traced onto template plastic, lightweight interfacing, tracing paper, or acetate. The overlay is then placed over your background fabric to accurately position appliqué pieces.

Pin basting: Using pins to temporarily hold fabric in place.

Seam allowance: The extra fabric outside the finished appliqué shape. The standard appliqué seam allowance is ¼" on all sides of an appliqué piece. Sometimes the directions may call for a skimpy or generous ¼" seam allowance. This means to make your seam allowance just a little narrower or wider than ¼".

Straight grain: The threads that run the length (lengthwise grain) and width (crosswise grain) of the fabric.

Template: An appliqué shape cut from plastic or cardboard and used as a pattern for tracing a design onto fabric or paper. Cut appliqué templates the finished size of the shape and do not include seam allowances.

Window template: A shape cut in a piece of paper that lets you preview fabric choices or correctly position layered appliqué pieces.

Appliqué Supplies

THESE ARE MANY of the products available in quilt and fabric shops that will help you successfully complete your appliqué projects.

Needles: When you choose a needle for hand appliqué, size is very important. A sharp, fine needle glides easily through the edge of appliqué pieces, creating small, invisible stitches. In needle sizes, the higher the number, the finer the needle. Use sizes 10–12 for best results.

Some appliqué stitchers use short quilting needles called Betweens because they feel that short needles give them greater control. Official appliqué needles are longer and are called Sharps. An even longer needle called a Straw or Milliner's works well for needle turning the appliqué edge as you stitch it to the background. Try different needles to find the one most comfortable for you.

Between ====================
Sharp ====================
Milliner's ====================

Needles for machine appliqué are thinner than all-purpose needles. Each time you start a project, put a new size 75/11 or 70/10 needle in your sewing machine.

Thread: Appliqué thread should match the color of the appliqué fabric rather than the background fabric. Appliqué designs with many different-colored pieces require many shades of thread. If it is not possible to match the color exactly, choose thread that is a little darker than the fabric. For appliqué fabrics that are printed with many colors, choose a thread that blends with the predominant color. Sometimes a neutral brown or gray blends perfectly.

The best thread for stitching appliqués is 100% cotton. It is pliable and blends invisibly into the edges of the appliqués. If you can't find cotton thread in just the right color, use cotton-covered polyester thread. Size 50 is all-purpose sewing thread and can be found in all sewing stores. Size 60 is a finer thread which helps make your stitches invisible. Some hand stitchers also love to use thin silk thread. Invisible monofilament or rayon thread is an option for decorative machine appliqué and quilting. Experiment and see which thread you like best.

Always use white or light-colored thread for basting. Dye from dark thread can leave small dots of color on light fabrics.

Needle threader: If a needle is difficult to thread, use a needle threader to insert the thread through the eye of the needle.

Pins: Small ½" or ¾" straight pins are wonderful for pin basting because they do not catch the thread as you stitch.

Scissors: Small scissors with sharp blades that cut all the way to the point are often a stitcher's prized possession. You will also need scissors to cut paper, cardboard, or plastic templates.

Thimble: Use a thimble to protect your finger as you push the needle through your fabric for hand appliqué.

Glue stick: A water-soluble glue stick is handy for glue basting seam allowances and basting appliqué pieces to the background fabric.

Fabric markers: Choose from a variety of fabric markers to trace appliqué designs onto the background fabric and to mark appliqué pieces. Use silver marking pencils, water-erasable pens, or fine-lead mechanical pencils for light fabrics. For dark fabrics, use sharp chalk pencils in white or yellow. It is always wise to test the markers on a scrap of fabric to make sure the marks can be easily removed.

Template plastic and permanent marker: Use template plastic to make patterns for the appliqué pieces. Cardboard templates are an option, but plastic templates are more durable and accurate. You can iron templates made from heat-resistant plastic. Use a fine-tipped permanent marker to trace the designs onto the plastic.

Plastic multi-circle stencil: Found in most office and art supply stores, this handy stencil makes perfect circles.

Freezer paper: Freezer paper is available at most grocery stores and quilt shops. The shiny, plastic-coated side softens and sticks to fabric when you apply a dry, warm iron to the uncoated side. Use freezer paper to make templates for freezer-paper appliqué techniques.

Tweezers: A small pair of tweezers makes it easy to remove freezer paper after you have appliquéd a piece to the background.

Iron: Use a steam iron to press your fabric before you appliqué. Use a dry iron to attach freezer-paper templates to your fabric. Press finished blocks with a steam iron.

Tape: Use Scotch Removable Magic Tape to anchor your fabric to your pattern while you trace the design onto your background fabric. Unlike other tapes, Scotch Removable will not rip the paper or fray your fabric.

Plastic bags: What did we do before zip-top bags were invented? They keep your appliqué pieces organized and clean.

Your favorite chair and lamp: When you hand appliqué, you will be more comfortable and make smaller stitches if you sit in your favorite chair with a lamp aimed at your work.

Sewing machine: Machine appliqué requires a sewing machine that has a zigzag stitch and is in good working order.

Sewing machine feet: Use a ¼"-wide foot to sew accurate seams, an open-toe embroidery foot for machine satin stitches, and a walking foot for machine quilting.

Appliqué pillow: One of my favorite appliqué tools is a small pillow. I place it in my lap when I stitch. It makes it easy to see my work, rests my hands and shoulders, improves posture, and is a great pincushion.

1. Use a piece of 8½" x 11" notebook paper as a pattern.

2. Cut out two rectangles, one white fabric and one printed fabric, adding ¼" seam allowances to all sides.

3. Sew the rectangles right sides together using a ¼" seam allowance and leaving a 3" opening on one long side to turn the pillow.

Pillow Trim
Use purchased cording—or make your own—around the pillow edge to make the pillow sturdier.

4. Turn the pillow right side out and stuff firmly with Poly-fil.

5. Hand stitch the opening closed and enjoy your pillow!

Appliqué Fabrics

THE BEST PLACE to shop for appliqué fabrics is your favorite quilt shop. Take this book with you and you will find quilters who will help you choose just the right fabrics for your project.

Fabrics made of 100% cotton are easier to appliqué than synthetic fabrics, which fray more than cotton and are often slippery. Sometimes, however, the perfect fabric contains synthetic fibers, and it's worth a little extra care to use that fabric in your design.

When you choose fabrics for appliqué projects, you need fabric for two purposes: the background fabric and the appliqué pieces.

BACKGROUND FABRICS

Appliqué background fabrics are usually light, solid colors or small prints and stripes that complement the appliqué design. Avoid choosing prints or stripes that are too bold; they may make it difficult to see the appliquéd design.

White background fabrics add brightness and clarity to your appliqués. Off-white backgrounds enhance the richness of darker appliqué palettes. White-on-white prints are lovely choices for stitchers who prefer a subtle print rather than a solid background. A fabulous tea-dyed print can give an antique glow to quilts. Appliquéing onto a dark background creates a dramatic effect.

MOTIF FABRICS

To determine a color palette for your sampler quilt, choose a multicolored fabric printed with a design that reflects the theme of the quilt. This inspiration fabric makes a perfect border for your sampler, and you can select colors from it to use as the color scheme of your quilt. Sometimes fabrics have colored dots along the selvage, which can be used to choose coordinating fabrics for the appliqué pieces. Choose fabrics for your appliqué pieces that are appropriate for the design. Consider the proper color and print size for the pattern you are stitching. Think about the designs you are "painting" with fabric.

Printed fabrics make your designs exciting. They also help conceal your stitches along the appliqué edges. Fabric printed in different values of one color can be very effective for flowers and leaves. These tone-on-tone fabrics, such as dark green printed over a lighter green, look like a solid but with a subtle texture. In addition, the designs of printed fabrics may contain lines that can be used to emphasize veins in leaves or textures in flower petals.

Fabrics printed with flowers and leaves are wonderful to use in appliqué because you can fussy cut whole flowers or individual petals and leaves to add realism to your appliqués (see "Fussy Cutting" on page 14). Use basket-weave prints for baskets or wood-grain prints for stems. Nature prints provide fabrics with water, sky, and leaves. Large-scale prints may seem inappropriate for appliqué, but a small piece cut from a specific area may make the perfect flower petal or bird wing.

You will also need fabric for the back of your sampler. Use a plain fabric or choose a print that coordinates with your sampler design. It's fun—and the print will hide your quilting stitches on the back.

FABRIC PASTE-UPS

How can you be sure you've chosen the right fabrics for your sampler? If you have enough fabric, make a pasteup of your colors before you start to stitch. Trace your pattern on a sheet of paper, cut the appliqué shapes out of your fabrics, and glue them to the design. Auditioning fabric in this manner helps you make decisions about color arrangements before you begin stitching. Use this as a placement guide for the fabrics when you stitch.

FABRIC PREPARATION

Prewash all fabric to preshrink it and to test for colorfastness. Wash dark and light colors separately. Sometimes it is necessary to wash and rinse dark-colored fabrics several times to get rid of excess dye. To test a fabric for colorfastness, cut a small piece, wet it, and place it on a scrap of background fabric. If color shows up on the background scrap, wash the fabric again, or choose a different fabric. Take the time to prewash your fabrics. This ensures that your finished quilt will not shrink and that the colors won't bleed onto each other when the quilt is laundered.

Press the fabrics to remove wrinkles so that you can accurately cut the appliqué and background pieces. Some quilters apply spray starch or sizing to help give the fabrics a little extra body.

Getting Ready to Appliqué

EFORE YOU APPLIQUÉ, you need to cut the background blocks, mark the appliqué placement lines, and make templates for the required appliqué pieces. Work carefully and accurately and your sampler will look great.

CUTTING BACKGROUND FABRIC

The sampler patterns in this book are all printed full size. The finished size of the center rectangle of each appliqué sampler is 9" x 12". Normally, the background fabric would be cut 9½" x 12½" to allow for ¼"-wide seam allowances on all sides. However, because appliqué blocks sometimes fray during stitching, cut the block 1" larger (10½" x 13½") and trim it to the correct size (9½" x 12½") after completing the appliqué. Cut accurate blocks and borders using a rotary cutter, mat, and acrylic ruler.

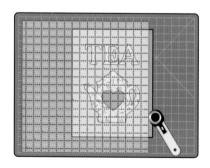

MARKING APPLIQUÉ PLACEMENT LINES

To accurately position the appliqué pieces onto the background fabric, mark the design directly onto the fabric.

To trace the design onto light background fabrics:

1. Place the background fabric right side up over the pattern so that the design is centered under the background piece. Tape your fabric over the pattern using removable tape.

2. Trace the design carefully. Use a silver marking pencil or a water-erasable pen to trace exactly on the lines. Test these markers on a scrap of fabric first to make sure you can remove the marks with cold water. If you are not certain that the marks will wash out, trace slightly inside the pattern lines. The lines will be covered by the appliquéd pieces after they are stitched, so you don't have to worry about removing the lines. Trace the design using solid or dotted lines. Some quilters prefer to use a minimal marking method for their appliqués. A single dot may denote placement for a circle; two dots may show placement for the ends of leaves.

To trace the design onto dark background fabrics:

1. Trace the design with a white or yellow chalk pencil.

2. Use a light box when you trace the design onto dark fabrics. If you do not have a light box, tape the pattern to a window or glass door on a sunny day. Center your fabric over the pattern, tape the fabric to the glass, and trace the design.

You can create your own light box by opening your dining room table and placing a storm window or sheet of Plexiglas over the table-leaf opening. Place a lamp or flashlight on the floor to shine through the glass like a light box. Place your pattern on the glass and your fabric on top of the pattern. The light will shine through so that you can easily trace your design.

PATTERN OVERLAY

If you find it difficult to trace the design onto your background fabric or if you do not wish to mark directly on your background fabric, try a pattern overlay. Some quilters prefer to use this technique when a pattern has many layers of appliqué pieces.

1. Make a pattern overlay by using a permanent marker to trace the pattern onto a piece of clear template plastic that is the same size as your background fabric. You can also use light-weight interfacing, tracing paper, or acetate.

Perfect Overlays
Photocopy or scan your design onto a sheet of clear acetate to make a fast and accurate overlay.

2. Place the plastic over the background fabric. To position each appliqué piece, lift up the plastic, slide each piece under the appropriate marking, then pin or baste the appliqué to the background fabric.

Slide appliqué shapes under the overlay to place them on the background.

MAKING APPLIQUÉ TEMPLATES

Trace the pieces of each appliqué design directly from the pattern to create the templates you need. Prepare your templates accurately to ensure the best results.

Making and Using Plastic Templates
Make templates for the appliqué pieces by using a fine-tipped marker to trace the appliqué design pieces onto template plastic. These durable templates can be used for most appliqué techniques.

1. Place the plastic over the pattern and trace each design piece with a fine-tipped permanent marker. Do not add seam allowances.

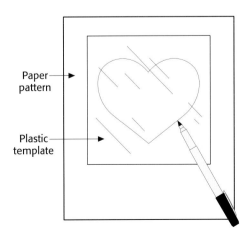

Paper pattern

Plastic template

2. Cut out the templates on the traced lines so they are the exact size of the original pieces.

3. Label the front of each template with the pattern name and template letter. This is the right side of the template.

If a design is repeated in a quilt, you only need one plastic template for each design. For example, you need one heart template to make the four hearts in the sampler borders on pages 94 and 95.

To use your plastic templates, follow these instructions:

1. Place the plastic template right side up on the right side of the fabric. Place a sheet of fine sandpaper under your fabric to prevent the fabric from slipping as you work. A small piece of double-sided tape on the back of the template will also keep it in place.

2. Trace around the template, marking on the right side of the fabric. Use a pencil or an appropriate marker for your fabric. When you trace pieces onto your fabric, leave at least ½" separation between pieces.

3. Cut out each fabric piece, adding a ¼"-wide seam allowance to all sides. The seam allowance will be turned under to create the finished edge of the appliqué.

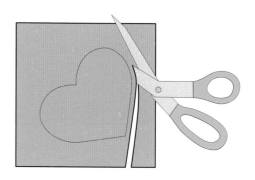

Making and Using Freezer-Paper Templates
Use freezer-paper templates for all freezer-paper appliqué techniques. Make freezer-paper templates by tracing the designs directly onto the freezer paper. For repeated designs, make a plastic template and trace around it onto the freezer paper. This helps ensure that your freezer-paper pieces are all the same size.

1. Place the freezer paper, coated side down, over the design, and trace the design onto the paper side with a fine-lead mechanical pencil.

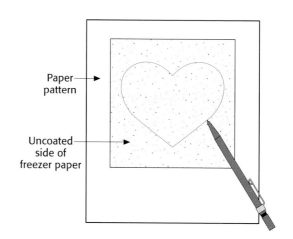

2. Cut out the templates on the traced lines so that they are the exact size of the design pieces.

Reverse Images

Trace symmetrical designs directly from the pattern to the paper. For asymmetrical designs, like the teapot on page 80, you must trace a reverse (mirror) image of the pattern piece. To trace a reverse image, turn the pattern over and place it on a light box or against a bright window, and trace the pattern pieces onto the freezer paper.

3. Cut multiple layers of freezer paper for repeated pieces by stapling up to four layers of freezer paper together. First, trace the design onto the top layer and then place your staples in the space that will be cut away. The staples hold the layers together as you cut accurate templates.

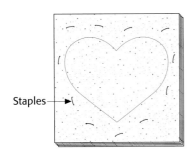

Staples

Use freezer-paper templates either on the top or on the back of the appliqué fabric.

Freezer Paper on Top:

1. For this method, trace all shapes onto freezer paper as they appear on the pattern. Do *not* trace asymmetrical designs in reverse.

2. Place the freezer-paper template with the coated side facing the right side of the appliqué fabric. Leave at least ½" between pieces.

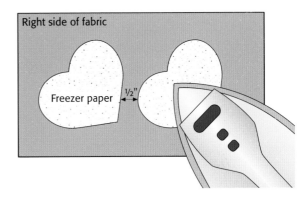

Right side of fabric

Freezer paper   ½"

3. Press the freezer paper to the right side of the fabric using a hot, dry iron. Let the piece cool.

4. Cut out the fabric appliqué piece, adding a ¼"-wide seam allowance around the outside edge of each freezer-paper shape.

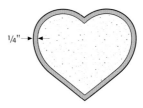

¼"

Label Templates

You can also cut your appliqué shapes from removable self-stick labels—they stick well and can be reused several times.

Freezer Paper on Back:

1. For this method, asymmetrical shapes must be traced in reverse. See "Making and Using Freezer-Paper Templates" on page 12.

2. Place the freezer-paper template with the coated side facing the wrong side of the appliqué fabric. Leave at least ½" between pieces.

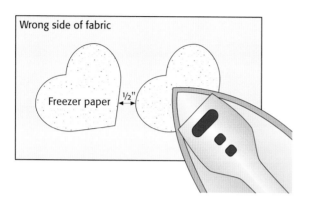

3. Press the freezer paper to the wrong side of the fabric using a hot, dry iron. Let the piece cool.

4. Cut out the fabric appliqué piece, adding a generous ¼"-wide seam allowance around the outside edge of each freezer-paper shape.

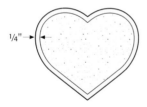

Placing Templates on the Fabric

Here is some information to help you choose the perfect section of your fabric for each appliqué shape. Your appliqué will be more beautiful if you carefully consider where to cut.

Grain lines: Appliqué designs do not usually provide grain lines to aid in positioning the templates on the fabric. If possible, place the templates on the appliqué fabric so that the grain runs in the same direction as the background fabric.

Designs that have inside points (such as hearts) or curves (such as leaves) should be placed on the bias. The bias prevents fraying at inside points and helps ease fabric around curves.

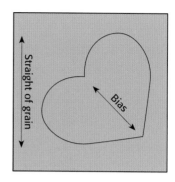

Fussy cutting: For some designs, you can cut an appliqué piece to include a specific part of a printed fabric. Quilters love to fussy cut leaves or flowers printed on the fabric. In this case, disregard grain lines and enjoy the way that the fabric and the appliqué design work together.

Window template: To get a special effect from a fabric, trace the appliqué piece onto paper and cut it out to create a window template. Move the window over your fabric to determine the perfect placement for your template before you cut out the appliqué piece.

Preparing Appliqué Pieces

THERE ARE MANY techniques for preparing appliqué fabric pieces before sewing. Preparation means that you need to turn under the raw edges of each appliqué shape, baste or glue the seam allowances, and pin or baste the appliqué pieces to the background fabric. You can choose different ways to prepare your own appliqué pieces. Some methods work better than others in particular situations and with specific fabrics. These techniques can also be used with machine appliqué but specific machine preparation methods are covered in "Machine Appliqué" on page 37. These methods are all correct and successful. You will probably like one better than others but try them all, and then choose your favorite!

METHOD ONE: TRADITIONAL APPLIQUÉ PREPARATION

When I first learned to appliqué, this is the method I used. You don't need any special tools, just templates, fabric, needle, and thread.

1. Cut out the appliqué shapes referring to "Making and Using Plastic Templates" on page 11.

2. Turn under the seam allowances by rolling the seam under a short segment at a time as you stitch. Roll the traced line to the back of the appliqué piece so it doesn't show on the front of the appliqué. Clip any inside points if necessary.

3. Hand baste the seam allowance in place, using light-colored thread in your needle. Refer to "Hand-Basting Primer" on page 20.

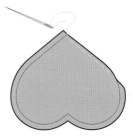

4. Pin or baste the appliqué to the background fabric and stitch it in place. Refer to "Hand Appliqué" on page 23.

METHOD TWO: GLUE-STICK PREPARATION

A water-soluble glue stick allows you to substitute glue basting for hand basting. Using glue saves time when preparing the pieces for appliqué, and the glue washes out after the stitching is finished. Be sure to prewash your fabrics if you choose this method because you will be soaking the fabric to get the glue out and you don't want your colors to run.

1. Cut out appliqué shapes referring to "Making and Using Plastic Templates" on page 11.

2. Apply glue stick to the ¼"-wide seam allowance on the wrong side of the appliqué. Try not to get too much glue in the fold area of the seam allowance or it will make the edges stiff and difficult to stitch in place.

3. Wait a few seconds for the glue to get tacky; then carefully fold the seam allowance to the back of the appliqué piece. Roll the traced line to the back of the appliqué piece so it doesn't show on the front of the appliqué. Clip any inside points if necessary.

Fold.

4. On the background fabric, apply glue to the center of the appliqué location. Position the appliqué on the background fabric, finger-press into place, and allow the glue to dry. Stitch it in place referring to "Hand Appliqué" on page 23.

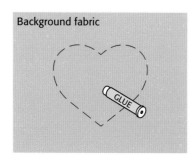

Background fabric

5. When you are finished stitching all the appliqués in place, soak the project in warm, soapy water to remove the glue. After the piece is dry, press from the wrong side.

METHOD THREE: FREEZER PAPER ON BACK AND BASTED PREPARATION

This is my favorite method! Freezer paper sticks to the fabric and controls the appliqué shape. I like to use this method when I want accuracy in repeated designs.

1. Cut out the appliqué shapes referring to "Freezer Paper on Back" on page 14. Add a generous ¼" seam allowance when cutting out the shapes.

2. Turn the ¼" seam allowance toward the freezer paper and baste by hand or use a glue stick to baste it to the paper. Clip any inside points to within a few threads of the freezer paper and fold the outside points.

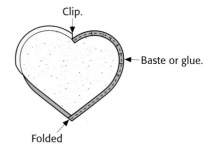

Clip.

Baste or glue.

Folded

3. Pin or baste the appliqué to the background fabric and stitch it in place referring to "Hand Appliqué" on page 23.

4. After stitching the appliqués in place, remove any basting stitches. Cut a small slit in the background fabric behind the appliqué and remove the freezer paper with tweezers.

Wrong side of background

If you have basted with a glue stick, soak the piece in warm water for a few minutes to soften the glue and release the paper. Pull out the paper. After the appliqué dries, press it from the wrong side.

METHOD FOUR: NEEDLE-TURN APPLIQUÉ PREPARATION

This preparation method saves time because you do not baste the seam allowances. Use your needle to control the fabric, and be careful not to pull the thread too tightly. Use this preparation method with "Needle-Turn Appliqué" on page 27.

1. Cut out the appliqué shapes referring to "Making and Using Plastic Templates" on page 11. Add a skimpy ¼" seam allowance when cutting out the shapes.

2. Place the appliqué pieces on the background fabric and pin or baste them securely in place. Position the appliqué as accurately as possible; the seam allowances should overlap the background markings.

3. Appliqué the shapes in place referring to "Needle-Turn Appliqué" on page 27.

METHOD FIVE: NEEDLE-TURN PREPARATION USING FREEZER PAPER

This technique uses freezer paper for accurate shaping, but eliminates the basting step. Use this preparation method with "Needle-Turn Appliqué" on page 27.

Creating Appliqué Shapes with Paper on Back

1. Cut out the appliqué shapes referring to "Freezer Paper on Back" on page 14. Clip any inside points, but do not turn under and baste the seam allowances to the wrong side.

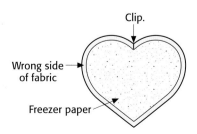

Clip.

Wrong side of fabric

Freezer paper

2. Place the appliqué pieces on the background fabric and position the appliqué as accurately as possible; the seam allowances should overlap the background markings. Pin or baste them securely in place.

3. Appliqué the shapes in place referring to "Needle-Turn Appliqué" on page 27. The stiffness of the freezer paper makes it easy to turn under the seam allowances and gives you a smooth edge to work against. The result is a perfectly shaped finished appliqué.

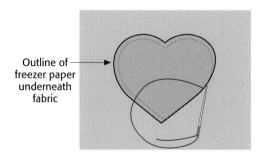

Outline of freezer paper underneath fabric

4. After stitching the appliqués in place, cut a small slit in the background fabric behind the appliqué and remove the freezer paper with tweezers.

Creating Appliqué Shapes with Paper on Top

If you do not like the idea of cutting the back of your work after you appliqué to remove the freezer paper, try ironing the freezer paper to the right side of your appliqué fabric.

1. Cut out shapes referring to "Freezer Paper on Top" on page 13.

2. Securely pin or baste the appliqué to the background fabric.

3. Following the shape of the paper, use the tip of your needle to gently turn under the seam allowance, referring to "Needle-Turn Appliqué" on page 27. Turn under the seam allowance at the edge of the freezer paper so that the fold shows just beyond the edge of the paper. Use the tip of the needle to smooth the fabric along

the edge; then stitch the appliqué to the background fabric.

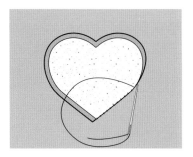

4. Peel away the freezer paper when you are finished.

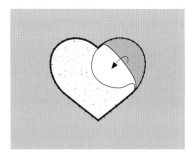

METHOD SIX: STITCH-MARKED APPLIQUÉ PREPARATION

This method provides perfect placement for appliqué pieces. It's a wonderful method for keeping appliquéd letters on a straight line. Try it!

1. Trace the appliqué design on the wrong side of the *background* fabric with a sharp pencil. Refer to "Reverse Images" on page 13 to trace asymmetrical shapes in reverse.

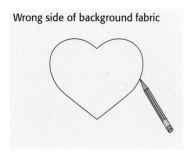

Wrong side of background fabric

2. Cut a piece of appliqué fabric slightly larger than the desired shape. Place the background fabric against a light source and place the appliqué fabric over the marked design. The wrong side of the appliqué fabric should be next to the right side of the background fabric. Pin the appliqué fabric in place.

3. Turn the background fabric to the wrong side and sew running stitches along the pencil line, stitching through both layers of fabric. Use a large needle and heavy thread (quilting thread) to make perforations in the fabrics. Begin and end with a single knot.

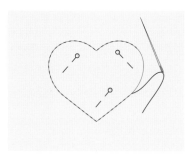

4. On the right side of the appliqué fabric, trim around the appliqué design, adding a skimpy ¼" seam allowance around the edge of the stitched design.

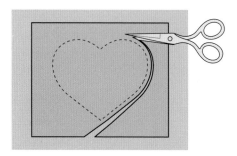

5. Use your small, sharp scissors to clip every third stitch for about 2".

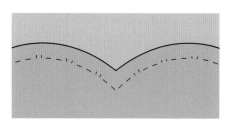

6. Pick out the clipped threads in the first clipped section, needle turn the seam allowance, and appliqué referring to "Needle-Turn Appliqué" on page 27. The perforations from the basting stitches will help to turn the edges of the appliqué fabric and mark the placement line on the background.

7. Continue removing the clipped threads and stitching the appliqué to complete the design.

METHOD SEVEN: LINED APPLIQUÉ PREPARATION

When you are appliquéing light-colored shapes, such as the "Bloom" fence on page 58 or the "Peace" doves on page 72, you can use fusible lightweight interfacing to line your pieces so that the background will not show through the appliqué pieces.

1. Place the interfacing on top of your pattern with the fusible side down and trace the design using a sharp pencil. Refer to "Reverse Images" on page 13 to trace asymmetrical shapes in reverse.

2. Cut out the interfacing on the pencil line. Do not add seam allowances.

3. Place the fusible side of the interfacing against the wrong side of the appliqué fabric. Iron the interfacing in place following the manufacturer's directions.

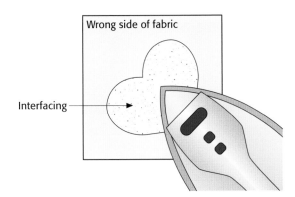

4. Cut out the appliqué, adding a ¼"-wide seam allowance of fabric around the outside edge of the interfacing.

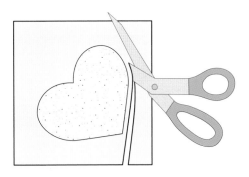

5. Turn the ¼" seam allowance toward the interfacing and baste by hand or use a glue stick. Clip any inside points and fold the outside points.

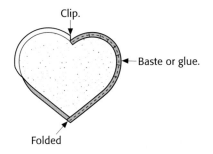

6. Pin or baste the appliqué to the background fabric and stitch it in place referring to "Hand Appliqué" on page 23.

7. Remove any basting stitches. Leave the interfacing inside to line the appliqué.

Hand-Basting Primer

ERE ARE MY favorite tips for hand basting the seam allowances of appliqué shapes. Practice basting the edges of a heart-shaped appliqué and you will feel confident stitching straight edges, curves, and points.

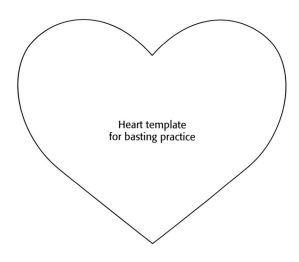

Heart template
for basting practice

1. Cut out the heart shape referring to "Making and Using Freezer-Paper Templates" on page 12 and "Freezer Paper on Back" on page 14.

2. Thread a needle with an 18" length of light-colored thread. Avoid dark-colored thread that can leave spots of dye on your fabric. Do not make a knot in the end; this makes it easier to remove the basting thread later.

STRAIGHT EDGES

1. Instead of starting with a knot, leave a little tail of thread when you start. The paper will hold the thread in place.

2. Begin at the point and turn under the straight edge of the heart. Hand baste the heart along the straight edge, folding the seam allowance snugly over and against the freezer-paper heart. Sew through the two layers of fabric and the freezer paper.

3. Look at the right side of the piece while you turn under the fabric and baste. Check that you are maintaining a smooth edge. If you keep your stitches near the fold, you will be sure to catch the seam allowance underneath.

4. Stop about halfway up one side of the heart.

OUTSIDE CURVES

1. Baste outside curves by making small running stitches in the seam allowance only. Do not baste through the paper and the right side of the fabric. Gently pull the thread to gather the fabric and ease the seam allowance around the curve for a smooth fit.

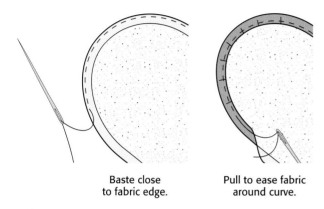

Baste close to fabric edge.

Pull to ease fabric around curve.

2. Do not clip the outside curve because clipping creates little bumps along the edge of the appliqué.

3. If little points appear along the curve, you can control them with the tip of your needle when you sew the appliqué to the background.

INSIDE POINTS

1. As you finish basting the first curve of your heart, you will come to the inside point, also known as the cleavage. Carefully clip the seam allowance straight into the cleavage to allow the fabric to turn under easily. Stop clipping about four to five threads away from the freezer paper. Do not clip all the way into the point.

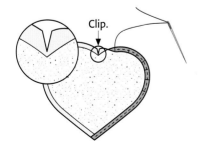

Clip.

2. Use a pencil to mark two Xs on the back of your freezer-paper heart as shown.

3. As you baste the inside point, try this "wonder stitch" to prevent fraying at the clipped point and keep the basting thread away from the inside point while you appliqué.

   Take a stitch from the clipped edge into the closest X on the back of the heart through to the right side of the fabric. This will gently pull the seam allowance away from the inside point.

Bring the needle back up through the other X. This keeps the thread away from your appliqué stitches at the inside point.

Pull the seam allowance of the second curve snugly over the freezer paper. Insert the needle into the seam allowance and begin basting the second curve, gathering the fullness of the second curve.

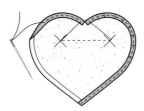

This stitch should "lift and separate" the seam allowance and enhance the cleavage.

4. If there are threads fraying at the inside point, do not force them to turn under. These can be pushed under with the tip of the needle when you appliqué. See "Inside Points" on page 29.

OUTSIDE POINTS

1. As you get to the outside point of the heart, finger-press the remaining seam allowance under. Turn the end over the beginning to form a clean point and baste in place. A small tab of fabric may show on the edge, but you can tuck it under with your needle when you appliqué. This method works great when you can begin and end at the same point.

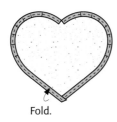

Fold.

2. There is another good method for preparing outside points. Begin by turning the point of the fabric in toward the appliqué. Apply a small

dab of glue stick to hold this in place. Fold the right side under, then the left, to form a sharp point. This technique also works well on leaves.

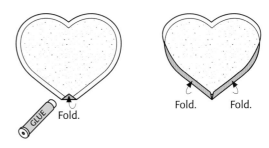

Fold.   Fold.   Fold.

The seam allowances may overlap slightly at the point. They will overlap more on a very sharp point. If the fabric at the point is too thick to baste where the seam allowances cross, push the extra fabric under the point with your needle later when you sew. Baste close to the edge.

INSIDE CURVES

The only basic shape not included in the heart is an inside curve. An inside curve should be clipped in several places (every ¼") so that the seam allowance will relax and turn under smoothly. Clip only halfway through the seam allowance to avoid fraying at the edge of the appliqué.

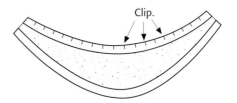

Clip.

ONE LAST THING

When you finish basting your appliqué shape, don't tie a knot. Leave a thread tail and you will be able to remove your basting threads easily.

Hand Appliqué

You've cut out your appliqué pieces and prepared the seam allowances. It's time to thread your needle and appliqué!

BASTING APPLIQUÉS TO THE BACKGROUND

Now that your appliqué shapes are cut and the seam allowances are basted, you are ready to baste the shapes to the background fabric. This will hold them in place while you appliqué.

Pin Basting

Most stitchers pin baste their appliqués in place one or two pieces at a time. Use several pins to attach the appliqué pieces to the background so that they will not slip out of place. Small ¾" sequin pins are wonderful because they do not get in the way of the thread as you stitch.

If you do have trouble with threads tangling around the pins as you sew, pin the appliqués in place from the wrong side of the background fabric.

Glue Basting

Baste the pieces in place using a water-soluble glue stick. Apply glue stick to the background fabric, keeping glue toward the center of the piece. Do not apply glue along the outer edges where you will stitch because the glue will stiffen the fabric and make it difficult to sew the appliqué to the background.

After applying the glue, position the appliqué and wait for the glue to dry before sewing. You should soak the appliqué in warm water when you are finished to remove the glue.

Hand Basting

Basting by hand is another option. Using light-colored thread, baste near the edges of the appliqués.

THREADING THE NEEDLE AND TYING A KNOT

Before you stitch your appliqués to the background fabric, take a few minutes to learn some important information about thread.

- Color is very important. If you match the thread color to your appliqué fabric, it will blend in and your stitches will seem smaller and almost invisible. If you can't find the perfect color match, use thread that is a little darker. It will blend into the appliqué fabric. A lighter shade of thread may sparkle and show along the edge.
- Cut a single strand of thread about 18" long. If your thread is too long, it will tangle and you will have unwanted knots.
- Use a new thread for each appliqué piece. It's tempting to use every inch of your thread, but it frays and loses strength with repeated stitching.
- Thread is smoother in one direction because it is twisted when it is manufactured. You can take advantage of this by cutting and knotting your thread so it will slide smoothly through the fabric.

  If you are right-handed, thread the needle before you cut the thread off the spool. Then cut the thread near the spool and tie a knot in the end that you cut.

  If you are left-handed, tie a knot in the end of the thread while it is still on the spool. Then measure off 18". Cut the thread near the spool and thread the cut end into the needle. No more twisted threads while you stitch!

- If you have trouble threading the needle, trim the end of the thread at an angle with sharp scissors.
- Try putting the needle onto the thread instead of the thread through the needle. Surprise!

Move the needle toward the thread.

To make a quilter's knot in the end of your thread:

1. Hold the needle in your sewing hand and the end of the thread in your other hand.

2. Cross the tail of thread in front of the needle, and hold the thread securely between your forefinger and thumb.

Hold thread between thumb and forefinger.

3. Move the thread away from you, wrapping the thread around the needle three times.

Wrap thread around needle three times.

4. Hold the wrapped thread between your finger and thumb and gently pull the needle through the wraps.

Pull needle through wraps.

5. A neat knot will appear at the end of your thread.

TRADITIONAL APPLIQUÉ STITCH

The traditional appliqué stitch is appropriate for sewing all areas of your appliqué designs. It works well on straight areas as well as on sharp points and curves.

1. Thread your needle with a single strand of thread approximately 18" long. Tie a knot in one end. To hide your knot as you begin, slip your needle into the seam allowance from the wrong side of the appliqué piece (but not through the background fabric), bringing it out through the fold line. The knot will be hidden inside the seam allowance and your work will look very tidy.

2. Stitch along the outer edge of the appliqué. If you are right-handed, stitch from right to left. If you are left-handed, stitch from left to right. Start the first stitch by bringing your needle straight out of the appliqué and inserting it into the background fabric directly opposite where the thread exited the appliqué.

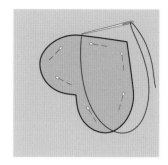

3. Move the needle forward about ⅛" under the background fabric to take a stitch parallel to the edge of the appliqué. Then bring it through to the right side of the background fabric, right at the edge of the appliqué. As you continue, pierce the edge of the appliqué piece, catching only one or two threads of the folded edge.

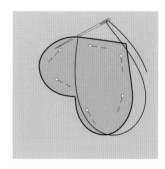

Stitch Support

Support your fabric by holding the pointer finger or middle finger of your non-sewing hand directly under the appliqué. As you stitch, push the needle underneath until it gently touches your finger; then move the needle back up through the fabric.

4. Bring the needle straight off of the appliqué edge and back into the background fabric. Let your needle travel forward another ⅛" under the background, bringing it up again to barely catch the edge of the appliqué.

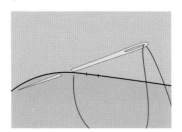

Give the thread a slight tug and continue stitching. The only visible parts of the stitch are small dots of thread along the appliqué edge.

The part of the stitch that travels forward will be seen as a ⅛"-long stitch on the wrong side of the background fabric.

Wrong side of fabric

Stitching Tips

- *As you sew, keep your needle parallel to the appliqué edge with each forward stitch.*
- *Give the thread a slight tug so that it blends into the appliqué.*
- *Keep the length of your stitches consistent as you stitch along the straight edges. Make smaller stitches when you get to curves and points.*
- *And finally: Stop stitching while you still have enough thread to tie a final knot!*

5. When you get to the end of your appliqué stitching, or you are nearly out of thread, pull your needle through to the wrong side. Behind the appliqué piece, take two small stitches, making a simple knot by bringing your needle through the stitch loops.

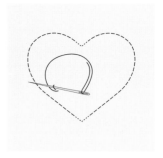

6. Before you cut your thread, take a moment to make the back of your work as neat as the front. Take one more small stitch behind the appliqué to direct the tail of the thread under the appliqué fabric. Clip the thread so that it won't show.

Clip here.

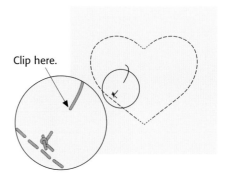

LADDER STITCH

The ladder stitch works well to invisibly appliqué straight areas and curves. However, when you stitch inside points or sharp outside points, you can switch to the traditional appliqué stitch to create more durable stitches.

1. Refer to page 24 to thread your needle and hide your knot.

2. Make a small stitch by moving your needle out of the appliqué edge and inserting the needle into the background fabric directly opposite where the thread exited the appliqué. Move the needle forward about ⅛" under the background fabric, taking a stitch parallel to the edge of the appliqué. Then bring it back up to the right side of the background fabric, right at the edge of the appliqué.

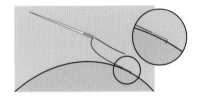

3. Insert the needle into the edge of the appliqué. Travel through the fold of the appliqué about ⅛" and bring the needle back out.

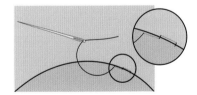

4. Insert the needle into the background fabric and repeat until you have taken five or six stitches. The visible stitches will resemble the rungs on a ladder.

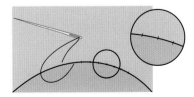

5. Pull lightly on the thread until the stitches disappear, attaching the appliqué neatly and invisibly to the background. The wrong side of your work will look like a running stitch, a series of stitches and spaces.

Wrong side of fabric

NEEDLE-TURN APPLIQUÉ

Use this technique after preparing the pieces according to methods four, five, and six on pages 17–19.

1. Beginning on a straight edge, use the tip of your needle to gently turn under the seam allowance about ½" at a time. Hold the turned seam allowance firmly between the thumb and first finger of your nonsewing hand as you stitch the appliqué securely to the background fabric.

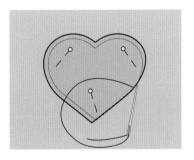

2. Stitch this ½" section to the background fabric, then needle turn the next ½" and repeat. A long milliner's or straw needle will help you to control the seam allowance and turn it under neatly. A round wooden toothpick can also help you turn under the seam allowance.

Appliqué Primer

CURVES, POINTS, STEMS, layered appliqué—all these elements require different techniques and stitches. Use this section to help you learn the best methods for all different parts of appliqué.

STRAIGHT EDGES

Straight edges are the easiest to appliqué, so this is a good place to concentrate on your basic appliqué stitches. Try to keep them straight, even, and consistent. Each stitch should be approximately ⅛" long.

OUTSIDE CURVES

As you stitch around an outside curve, try to keep the appliqué edge smooth. To keep little points of fabric from forming on the curves, push the seam allowance under with the tip of your needle, smoothing the folded edge before sewing. Keep your stitches a bit smaller so that these fabric points cannot escape between the stitches.

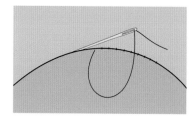

If you have sharp curves, use the basting technique on page 21 to ease the excess fabric into a smooth curve.

OUTSIDE POINTS

As you stitch toward an outside point, take smaller stitches within ½" of the point. Smaller stitches near the point keep any frayed edges of the seam allowance from escaping.

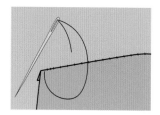

At the point, place the last stitch on the first side of the piece very close to the point. Take one extra lock stitch in the same place before you switch sides at the point. This extra stitch will hold your fabric securely as you turn the point and adjust the fabric on the second side.

Lock stitch

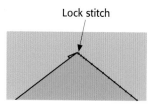

Place the next stitch on the opposite side of the point. A stitch on each side, close to the point, will accent the outside point. Do not put a stitch directly on the point because it might flatten the point.

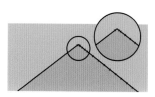

If a small tab of seam allowance extends beyond the edge of the appliqué, use your needle to push it under the appliqué before you stitch. Do not cut it off!

INSIDE POINTS

As you stitch toward an inside point (sometimes referred to as the cleavage), take smaller stitches within ½" of the point. Stop stitching ¹⁄₁₆" before you get to the inside point.

Before you stitch the inside point, use your needle to sweep any loose threads under the point. Place the tip of your needle ½" past the point and gently sweep the needle back to the point, pushing any frayed threads under the appliqué. A round wooden toothpick used in place of the needle will also help you sweep any fuzzies under the appliqué.

Sweep tip of needle under appliqué
and back toward inside point.

You're in Control!
A little dab of glue on your needle will control the fuzzies. Simply glide your needle over the top of your glue stick before you sweep the loose threads. This is my all-time favorite appliqué tip!

When you get to the deepest part of the point, use one large stitch to emphasize the point. Come up through the appliqué, catching a little more fabric in the stitch than normal—four or five threads from the fold instead of one or two. Make a straight stitch out over the edge of the appliqué, but insert your needle under the edge of the appliqué, pulling your needle through to the back side. With the needle underneath, pull the needle toward you. This will enhance the cleavage at the point!

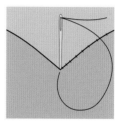

Insert needle
under appliqué edge.

If an inside point frays, use a few closely spaced stitches to tack the fabric down securely. If your thread matches the appliqué fabric, these stitches will blend in with the edge of the shape.

STEMS

There are several methods for creating appliqué stems. If the stems are straight, they can be cut on the straight grain of the fabric. If stems curve, they must be cut on the bias.

Stem Method One

This method is especially good for narrow stems.

1. Cut fabric strips that measure four times the finished stem width. For example, for a ¼" stem, cut the strips 1" wide.

2. Cut lengths ½" longer than the finished stem. This allows ¼"-wide seam allowances to be tucked under other appliqué pieces.

3. Fold the strip in half lengthwise, wrong sides together. Press with a steam iron or baste close to the raw edges.

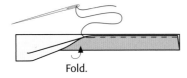

Fold.

4. Position the strip with the raw edges touching one of the marked stem lines. The folded edge of the stem should cover the other line. If the stems must curve, as in a wreath shape, position the raw edges of the strip just inside the *outer* curved line.

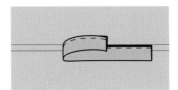

5. Using small running stitches, sew the strip to the background almost through the center of the strip—slightly closer to the raw edges than to the fold. Backstitch every few stitches to secure the stem to the background.

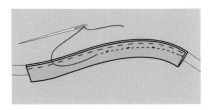

6. Roll the folded edge over the raw edges. Appliqué the fold to the background fabric to create a smooth stem.

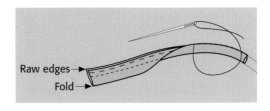

Raw edges →
Fold →

Stem Method Two

These neatly basted strips are great for wider stems.

1. Cut fabric strips that measure two times the finished stem width.

2. Cut lengths ½" longer than the finished stem. This allows ¼"-wide seam allowances to be tucked under other appliqué pieces.

3. Fold both raw edges in to meet at the center, wrong sides together. Baste along the folded edges using small running stitches.

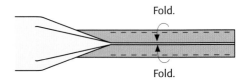

Fold.

Fold.

4. Center the stem, wrong side down, against the background fabric and pin or baste the stems to the background fabric. Appliqué along both folded edges. When a stem is long, I like to glue it to the background fabric to keep it in

place. On a sharp curve, stitch the inside edge first, then the outside edge. If you are making a curved stem or basket handle, pull gently on the inner basting thread and ease the fabric to create the curved stem.

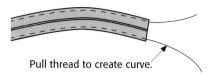

Pull thread to create curve.

5. Remove the basting threads after stitching is complete. You can also use a bias-tape maker to quickly make this same kind of stem without basting. Spray your strips with spray starch and feed them into the wide end of a bias-tape maker. Press the folded stems as they emerge from the narrow end of the tool.

Stem Method Three

You can use heat-resistant plastic or metal pressing bars, called bias bars, to make stems a uniform width. These are available at quilt shops in several sizes, from ⅛" to ½" wide. Choose the size that matches the finished width of the stems in your design.

1. Measure the width of the finished stem and cut *bias* strips twice this width plus ½" for seam allowances.

2. Fold the strip in half lengthwise, wrong sides together, and machine stitch a scant ¼" from the raw edges to make a tube. Slip the bias bar into the tube and position it with the seam centered on one side. Press the tube flat, with the seam allowance to one side. Be careful—the metal bars can get very hot. Push the bar through the tube to the other end. If necessary,

trim the seam allowance so it does not extend past the folded edge of the strip.

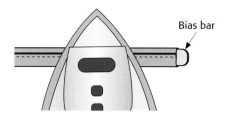

Bias bar

3. Remove the bar. Cut the tube into the required lengths for the stems (including seam allowances).

4. Position the stem on the background fabric with the seam allowance on the back. Pin or baste the stem to the background fabric and appliqué along both folded edges. On curved areas, stitch the inside curve in place first, then the outside curve.

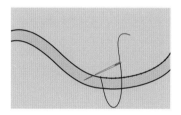

LEAVES

The curved edges of leaves will be easy to baste and stitch if the leaf is cut out on the bias. The curved bias edge will ease and create a smooth shape.

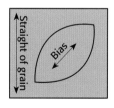

1. Fold, baste, and stitch sharp points on leaves like outside points on page 22.

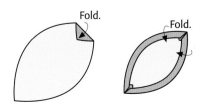

Fold.   Fold.

2. If a leaf is connected to a stem or flower, begin stitching at the connection. Take one or two stitches from the leaf to the stem so that they appear to be attached. Do not overlap the leaf and stem.

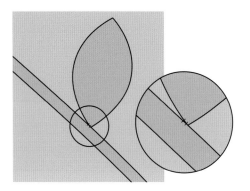

PERFECT CIRCLES

Use heavy paper, such as a manila folder, to cut circular templates. A plastic circle stencil, available in art stores, makes it easy to draw perfect circles.

1. Lay the circle stencil over the circle in your appliqué pattern to find the correct finished size for your design. Trace the circle onto heavy paper. Cut out the paper circle template, cutting as slowly and smoothly as possible. Use small, sharp scissors for best results. You can use a nail file to smooth the paper edge if necessary.

2. Use the circle stencil again to trace a circle onto your fabric. Make this circle ½" larger in diameter than the paper circle. This adds a ¼"-wide seam allow-ance around the outer edge of the design. Cut out the fabric circle.

Wrong side of fabric

Paper

¼"

3. Sew within the seam allowance with a small running stitch around the fabric circle, leaving at least 2" of thread at the beginning. Keep the stitches within the seam allowance, but not too close to the edge. Tie a single knot with the two thread ends and leave the thread ends loose.

4. Place the paper template in the center of the fabric circle. Pull the thread ends to draw the seam allowance around the template. You can pin the circle to the pad of your ironing board with a big straight pin so your hands will be free to pull the threads and adjust the fabric around the paper template.

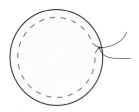

5. Steam press the circle, using spray starch if you like, then let it cool for a minute. Carefully peel back the fabric and remove the paper circle. Gently pull the basting threads to tighten the seam allowance again and make it lie flat. Tie another knot to secure the gathers and trim the threads.

6. Pin the circle to the desired location, and appliqué with smaller-than-usual stitches. For impressively small stitches, sew around the circle twice. The second time, place your stitches between the first ones.

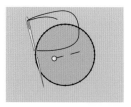

7. The paper templates that you remove before stitching are reusable. For larger circles, you can leave the paper inside the fabric until you have stitched the circle to the background. This helps to support the circle as you stitch. When you are finished, cut a little slit in the background behind the circle and pull the paper out with tweezers. Your circles will be very smooth.

Ready-Made Circles

You can also make circles by using office dots, which are available in a variety of sizes. They adhere to the right side of your fabric, enabling you to needle-turn appliqué the circle to the background fabric.

LAYERED APPLIQUÉ

Many appliqué designs contain elements that are overlapped or layered. Here are some tips for completing these designs.

Overlapped Pieces

If you look carefully at a design where two pieces touch, you will notice that one piece usually overlaps the other. When you plan your stitching for projects in this book, prepare the pieces in alphabetical order. If pieces overlap, do not turn under and stitch the seam allowance edges that will be covered by other pieces. As you appliqué, the raw edges of the first seam allowance will lie flat under the piece that covers it.

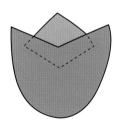

Layered Pieces

In addition to overlapping shapes, you will also find shapes that are layered on top of one another. When you appliqué the larger shape first, the positioning marks for the second piece disappear under the appliqué. An easy solution is to use a pattern overlay or simply make a window template as shown for perfect placement of the top piece.

1. Trace the two pattern pieces onto plain paper.

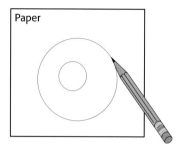

2. Cut out the larger design shape; then carefully cut out the inner shape to create a window.

Cut out to make a window.

3. Place the paper window over the first appliquéd piece. Position the second fabric piece through the window for perfect placement.

4. If you plan to quilt around the smaller layered shape, it helps to trim away the background fabric behind the larger shape after you appliqué it. Leave a ¼"-wide seam allowance inside the appliqué stitches then appliqué the smaller shape on top.

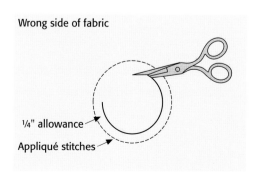

Wrong side of fabric

¼" allowance

Appliqué stitches

DIMENSIONAL TECHNIQUES

Once you have learned basic appliqué techniques, it's fun to add special touches with dimensional appliqué.

Folded Buds

This technique is used for the flower buds in the "Mom" sampler on page 70, the hanky in the angel's pocket in the "Believe" sampler on page 56, and the corner border pattern on page 93.

1. Cut a 2" square of fabric. Fold the square in half diagonally, wrong sides together.

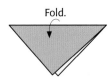

Fold.

2. Fold the point of each side down to the center point, overlapping the points so they are about ¼" away from the bottom point. Baste along the bottom edges of the bud.

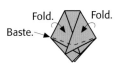

Fold. Fold.
Baste.

3. Appliqué the calyx (base of the bud), leaving the top edge unstitched. Insert the bud into the calyx using tweezers. Appliqué the top of the calyx, taking a few stitches all the way through to the background to secure the bud. The top of the bud is not stitched to the background.

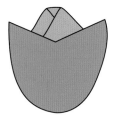

Yo-yos

Yo-yos are used for the wheels on the baby carriage in the "Baby" sampler on page 54.

1. Cut a 4¾"-diameter circle of fabric. For a great template, use a CD!

2. Turn under ¼" around the edge of the circle and, with a knotted thread, stitch with a running stitch near the fold. Use a double thread for strength.

3. Gather the edges together into the center of the circle. Tie a secure knot. Sew a few stitches back and forth across the opening, catching the edges on each side to close the hole. Finger-press the circle to make the edges smooth.

4. You can sew a button over the center hole, if desired, as shown in the "Baby" sampler on page 54.

Gathered Blossoms

Gathered blossoms are used for the geraniums in the "Bloom" sampler on page 58.

1. Cut a 2½"-diameter circle of fabric.

2. Turn under ⅛" and follow steps 2 and 3 of "Yo-yos" above.

3. Insert the needle straight down through the center of the gathers, bringing it through to the back (flat) side.

4. With the gathered side up, divide the circle into five equal flower petals as shown, marking lightly with a fabric marker.

5. To make the petals, bring the thread from the back over the outside edge of the flower (on the marked line) and insert it into the center again. Pull the thread to create a petal.

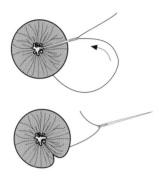

6. Continue looping the thread over the edges to make five petals. Knot the thread on the back of the flower; then tack the flower to the background fabric. Add three beads to the center.

Ruched Fabric

This technique is used for the angel's hair in the "Believe" sampler on page 56, the cake icing in the "Wish" sampler on page 88, and also the trim on the baby carriage in the "Baby" sampler on page 54.

1. Use a rotary cutter and ruler to cut a straight-grain strip of fabric 1⅛" wide and the length required in the pattern directions. Fold the long edges of the strip into the center of the strip so that the raw edges meet. Press.

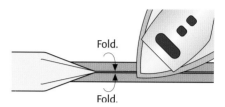

Fold.

Fold.

2. Lay the strip right side up along the ruching guide below. Use a fabric marker to place dots along both folded edges of your strip at 1" intervals. Start ¼" from one end with a secure knot and sew a zigzag running stitch from dot to dot. As you change directions, stitch over the folded edges.

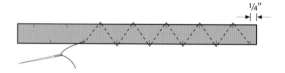

¼"

3. Pull the thread in a straight line, gathering fabric along each side. Stitch enough gathers to make a strip the correct length for your pattern.

4. If necessary, trim off the ends of the gathered strip, leaving just ¼" excess at both ends. Fold under these ¼" tails, arrange the gathers, and appliqué the edges of the strip in place referring to "Hand Appliqué" on page 23.

Ruching Guide

DECORATIVE STITCHES

Embroidery can add a decorative accent to your appliqué designs.

Use the outline or stem stitch with two strands of embroidery floss to embroider thin lines, such as flower stems and letters.

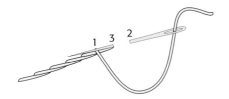

Outline or Stem Stitch

Use the chain stitch with two strands of embroidery thread to stitch the letters on the samplers. This gives a darker effect than the stem stitch.

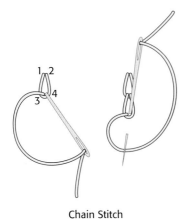

Chain Stitch

Use the buttonhole or blanket stitch to accent the edges of fusible appliqués.

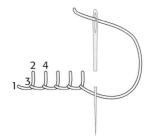

Buttonhole or Blanket Stitch

Machine Appliqué

HAND APPLIQUÉ IS a beautiful technique, but sometimes a quilter needs to get a project finished quickly. This is the time for machine appliqué. You can save a lot of time by attaching the appliqué pieces to the background fabric with easy machine stitches.

Before you begin, you'll need to get your sewing machine ready to appliqué:

- Make sure your machine is in good working order. Clean and oil it according to the manufacturer's directions. Sometimes lint in your machine can make the stitches skip.
- Insert a sharp, new needle. A smaller needle will help keep your stitches invisible along the edge of the appliqué. Use size 75/11 or 70/10.
- Use a clear foot or an open-toe foot so that you can see where you are stitching.

Open-toe foot

- For invisible stitches, thread the top of your machine with lightweight invisible monofilament thread. Use clear thread for light-colored fabrics and smoke-colored thread for darker fabrics. If you have trouble threading the needle with the invisible thread, use a dark permanent marker to mark the tip of the thread. Go to your quilt shop to purchase high-quality invisible thread—it makes a difference.

- Thread the machine bobbin with 60-weight thread in a color that matches your appliqué shape.
- Set your machine for a zigzag or blind hem stitch with the length and width set at approximately one mm.
- For all machine appliqué stitches, adjust the tension so it is slightly looser on top and test the stitch on scraps first. Bobbin thread should not show on the top of the fabric.
- Practice on a small sample before you start to machine appliqué your sampler.

MACHINE-APPLIQUÉ PREPARATION

The most successful method of machine-appliqué preparation is to use freezer-paper templates and a glue stick. Use the "Freezer Paper on Back" preparation method on page 14.

MACHINE STITCHES

There are several machine stitches you can use for machine appliqué. The first three are to be used for appliqués with turned-under edges.

Straight stitch: Use a straight stitch to sew close to the outer folded edge of the appliqué.

Zigzag stitch: Use a zigzag stitch to stitch on and off the folded edge of the appliqué.

Blind hem stitch: Use a blind hem stitch to sew two to five straight stitches on the background and then a zigzag into the folded edge of the appliqué.

Use the following two stitches for appliqués with fused edges. For preparation techniques, see "Fusible Appliqué" on page 39.

Buttonhole or blanket stitch: Use a decorative buttonhole or blanket stitch to simulate hand-embroidered edges.

Satin stitch: Use a satin stitch (or narrow zigzag stitch) to securely attach appliqués and add a nice finished edge.

STITCHING APPLIQUÉS USING A ZIGZAG STITCH

Before you start to sew, take a few stitches on a scrap of fabric so that you understand the position of the needle throughout the stitch sequence.

1. Position the appliqué under the sewing machine so that the needle will swing to the right. The needle should pierce the background fabric just off the edge of the appliqué.

Right swing position

2. As you stitch, the needle will swing to the left and pierce the folded edge of the appliqué piece.

Left swing position

3. Continue stitching around the appliqué piece. Be careful that the left swing of the needle always catches the appliqué edge. As you stitch around curves, take a few stitches at a time and turn the appliqué frequently. You might have to shorten the stitches at the inside or outside points.

4. When you get around to your starting place, stitch over your beginning stitches to hold your threads. You can clip the threads or pull them to the back and tie knots.

Fusible Appliqué

If you want to make a quick and easy project that is still beautiful, try fusible appliqué. In addition to the fabrics for the background and the appliqués, you will need a light-weight fusible-web product with a paper back, such as Steam-a-Seam 2, HeatnBond, or Wonder-Under.

Fusible webs are made of glue fibers adhered to a piece of release paper. When you place the fusible web against the wrong side of an appliqué shape and apply heat and pressure from an iron to the paper side, the web melts and adheres to the fabric. When you remove the paper backing, you can then iron the shape to the background fabric. When they cool, the melted fibers of the web form a thin, permanent bond between the fabrics.

For some fusible appliqué projects, you can simply cut and fuse the appliqué shapes in place onto the background fabric without any sewing. This is a good technique to use for the letters on the appliqué samplers.

Stitching by hand or machine around the edges of the appliqués makes them more durable, especially if you plan to wash your project. A lightweight, stitchable fusible web will hold the appliqués in place and eliminates any slipping and puckering while you sew. Depending on the stitch and the thread that you choose, the stitches can be either decorative or almost invisible.

BASIC FUSIBLE DIRECTIONS

These directions will give you a basic knowledge of fusible appliqué. When you purchase a fusible-web product, please take time to read the manufacturer's directions. Different products call for different heat settings and handling instructions.

1. Position the fusible web over the appliqué pattern with the paper side up. Use a pencil to trace each of the appliqué shapes separately onto the paper. Leave at least ½" between shapes. Trace symmetrical designs directly from the pattern to the paper. Asymmetrical shapes must be traced in reverse; see "Reverse Images" on page 13.

2. Cut the appliqué shapes from the fusible web, cutting approximately ¼" outside the marked line. This extra fabric is not a seam allowance. It just ensures that the glue will thoroughly cover the appliqué edges and helps the fabrics to fuse securely.

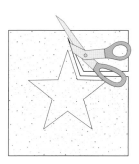

3. To prevent your appliqué shapes from becoming too stiff once they're fused, you can trim out the center of your fusible-web shapes. Leave at least ¼" inside the line. When you fuse the appliqués to the background fabric, the edges will be secure and the inner fabric will remain soft.

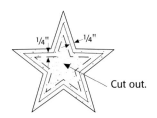

Cut out.

4. Place the shape, fusible-web side down, on the wrong side of the appropriate appliqué fabric. Following the manufacturer's directions, iron in place. Allow the shape to cool before handling.

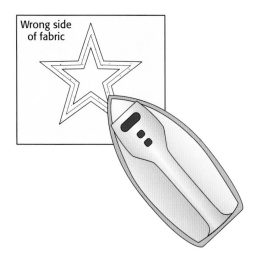

Wrong side of fabric

5. Now cut out the shape exactly on the drawn line.

6. Peel away the paper backing. If it is difficult to tear it away, tug gently to rip the paper so you can grasp the torn edge.

7. Arrange the fusible-backed appliqués in position on the right side of the background fabric and iron in place, following the manufacturer's directions. Allow the appliqué to cool before handling.

STITCHING FUSIBLE APPLIQUÉS

To create invisible stitches, use thread that matches the color of your appliqué fabric or invisible monofilament thread. For decorative stitches, use a contrasting color thread that will show.

Stitching Fusible Appliqués by Hand

Here are two hand stitches commonly used for securing the appliqué shapes to the background fabric.

1. Use two strands of embroidery floss.

2. The blanket or buttonhole stitch is a traditional stitch used to embellish the edges of these appliqués.

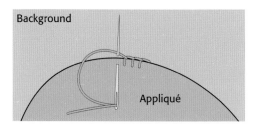

Background

Appliqué

3. The primitive stitch is a simple straight stitch, placed perpendicular to the edges of the appliqué. Bring your needle up through the appliqué (about ⅛" in from the edge); then take a straight stitch off the edge into the background fabric.

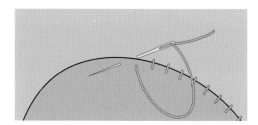

Stitching Fusible Appliqués by Machine

Here are two machine stitches commonly used for securing the appliqué shapes to the background fabric.

1. You can use either regular-weight or thinner embroidery-weight thread in your sewing machine. If you prefer invisible stitches, you can use mono-filament thread.

2. Some machines have decorative stitches designed to look just like the buttonhole stitch. Guide the fabric so that the straight stitch lies next to the appliqué and the left swing takes a stitch into your appliqué fabric. If your machine doesn't have this stitch, you can try to use the blind hem stitch to simulate the look.

3. A satin stitch completely covers the raw edge with stitches. Set the machine for a satin stitch using a short, narrow zigzag stitch. If you have adjusted the stitches correctly, they will be about ⅛" wide and very closely spaced without being piled on top of each other.

4. Place the appliqué under the needle and satin stitch over the raw edges. The right swing of the needle should penetrate the background fabric; the left swing of the needle should go through the appliqué. Make sure all raw edges of the appliqué are covered with stitches.

5. When you get around to your starting place, stop stitching in the background fabric. Pull the threads to the back and tie knots.

MACHINE SATIN-STITCHING TIPS

Place a piece of tear-away stabilizer on the wrong side of your work (or iron a piece of freezer paper on the back) to prevent puckering while you stitch. Remove after you have completed all of your machine stitching.

When stitching around curves, stop every few stitches with the needle down in the background fabric and lift the presser foot so you can turn the piece ever so slightly before taking the next few stitches.

To stitch an outside corner with secure, overlapping zigzag stitches:

1. Stitch the first side of the appliqué, ending at the outside corner with the needle down in the background fabric at the outside edge of the appliqué.

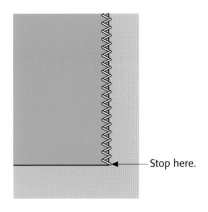

Stop here.

2. Raise the presser foot and pivot the fabric so you are ready to stitch the next side. Lower the presser foot as you begin to sew. The first few stitches will overlap the previous stitches at the corner.

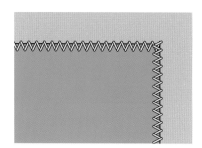

You can also stitch an outside corner with a mitered zigzag stitch. This produces a corner that isn't as thick as the overlapped corner above:

1. Repeat step 1 of the overlapped corner.

2. Raise the presser foot, pivot the fabric one half turn and take one diagonal stitch over the previous stitches ending with the needle in the background fabric. Using the wheel on your machine to manually position these stitches will be helpful.

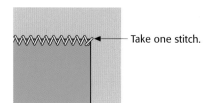

Take one stitch.

3. Raise the presser foot, pivot the fabric another half turn so that you are ready to stitch the next side, and continue stitching.

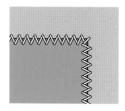

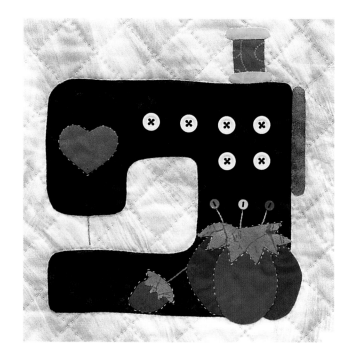

Finishing Your Sampler

C ONGRATULATIONS! YOU ARE ready to quilt your sampler and finish it with binding, a hanging sleeve, and a special label.

QUILTING

After you have completed your sampler top, quilting stitches outline and define your appliqué pieces. They can also create a design in the background area that adds a wonderful texture to your quilt.

Marking the Quilting Design

Mark the quilting designs before basting the three layers of the quilt together. Lay the quilt flat while marking it so that the lines will be smooth and accurate.

You can use a variety of tools to mark the quilting design onto the quilt top: a mechanical pencil, a silver marking pencil, a water-soluble pen, or a light-colored chalk pencil for dark fabrics. Whichever marking tool you use, test the tool on a scrap of your fabric before using it on your quilt. Make sure you can see the lines and that they can be removed.

To mark a quilting design, place the quilt top on top of the pattern and trace the design onto the fabric. Use a light box or tape your work against a window on a sunny day if you have trouble seeing the design through the fabric.

Many hand quilters mark a diagonal grid for their appliqué backgrounds. To mark this background quilting design, place dots at 1" intervals along the edges of the 9" x 12" block. Use a long

ruler to connect the dots and mark the diagonal lines.

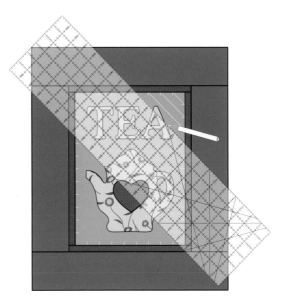

If you wish to quilt the borders, mark the border quilting lines 1" apart, using the dots marked in the center of the quilt as a guide.

Mark the corners with diagonal lines as shown.

If you don't want to mark the quilt prior to layering and basting, you can use masking tape to mark straight lines. Simply place the tape from dot to dot on the layered quilt and quilt along the edge of the tape. Peel the tape off with no marks to remove!

Machine quilters often use free-motion designs that do not need to be marked on the fabric either. Finally, you do not need to mark the quilting lines that outline the appliqués or the narrow inner borders. Referring to "Quilting Sequence" on page 45, simply quilt in the ditch along the edges.

Basting the Layers

Before you quilt, baste together the quilt top, batting, and backing. This secures the three layers and keeps the fabrics from slipping during the quilting process.

1. Press the quilt backing so that it is smooth. Cut the backing at least 4" larger than the quilt top.

2. Place the backing on a smooth surface, right side down. Use masking tape to fasten the corners and sides of the backing to the surface.

3. Place the batting on the backing, carefully smoothing it out. The batting should also be cut several inches larger than the quilt top.

4. Lay the quilt top, right side up, on the batting. Pin the three layers together in several places.

5. If you plan to hand quilt, baste the three layers together using a long needle and light-colored thread. Start in the center and baste a large X in the center of the quilt; then baste parallel lines to hold the layers together. The lines should be 3" to 4" apart. The more rows of basting you have, the better your layers will stay together. Finally, baste around the outside edges.

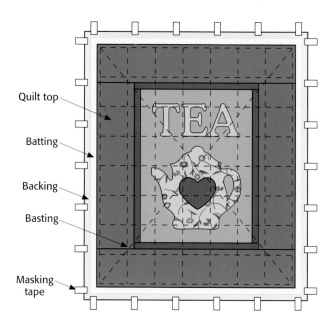

6. If you plan to machine quilt, use safety pins or a quilt-tack tool to baste the layers together at 3" to 4" intervals.

Hand Quilting

Hand quilting stitches are short running stitches used to sew the three layers of your quilt together.

1. Thread a Between needle with an 18" length of hand-quilting thread and tie a single knot in the long end of the thread. Insert the needle through the top layer of the quilt about ¾" away from the point where you want to start stitching. Slide the needle through the batting layer (not through the backing) and bring the needle out at the starting point.

2. Gently tug on the thread until the knot pops through the fabric and is buried in the batting. Take a stitch and begin quilting, making small running stitches that go equally through all layers. Take two, three, or four stitches at a time, trying to keep them straight and even.

3. To end a line of quilting, make a single knot approximately ¼" from your quilt top. Take a small backstitch into your quilt, through the top and batting only; then tug the knot into the batting and bring the needle out ¾" away from your stitches. Clip the thread even with the top and let the end disappear into your quilt.

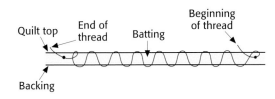

Batting for Hand Quilting

For easy hand quilting, I recommend a thin, low-loft cotton or polyester batting.

Machine Quilting

You can quilt quickly by machine. Adjust your stitch length to approximately 10 to 12 stitches per inch. Test your machine by stitching on a sample quilt sandwich (two layers of fabric with a scrap of batting between them) to make sure that the thread tension is even on the top and bottom.

Batting for Machine Quilting

A lightweight cotton batting or 80/20 blend is easy to handle when machine quilting.

Straight-Line Quilting

Use a walking foot or even-feed foot on your machine to stitch straight or slightly curved lines, to outline borders, or to quilt in the ditch. A walking foot helps to ease the top and bottom quilt layers evenly through the machine, creating smooth lines.

Walking or even-feed foot

Free-Motion Quilting

Machine quilters often use free-motion quilting to fill in the background areas or border areas. Use this technique to outline a motif or flower in the fabric, to stipple quilt, or to meander around the appliqués.

Use a darning foot and lower or cover the feed dogs on your machine so that you can freely move the fabric in the direction that you choose. Take a little time to sew a sample before you actually sew on your quilt.

 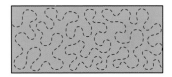

Darning foot

Quilting Sequence

1. Quilt closely around the outside edges of all appliqué pieces in the center design of your sampler. This is sometimes called quilting in the ditch.

2. Quilt in the ditch along the inner and outer edges of the narrow border. Your seam allowances should be pressed under the narrow border so that you are only quilting through one layer of fabric on the top of the quilt. Quilt against this seam ridge. Be careful to keep this line straight so that the quilt does not become distorted.

3. Quilt the background design in the center.

4. Quilt in the ditch around the border appliqué designs, if necessary.

5. Quilt the background design in the border.

HANGING SLEEVE

Sew a sleeve to the back of your quilt before you apply the binding. You can use this sleeve to hang your quilt on the wall with a rod.

1. For the projects in this book, cut a strip of fabric 6½" wide x 16½" long. This strip will make a 3"-wide sleeve.

2. Turn under ¼" twice at each short end of the strip and stitch a narrow hem.

3. Fold the sleeve lengthwise, wrong sides together, and pin the raw edges to the top of the quilt back. Machine baste ⅛" from the top edge. When you sew the binding to the quilt, the raw edge of the sleeve will be covered when the binding is turned to the back of the quilt.

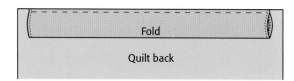

Fold

Quilt back

4. Pin the folded edge of the sleeve to the back of the quilt. Blindstitch the sleeve to the back of the quilt by hand, being careful not to stitch through to the front of the quilt.

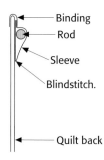

Binding
Rod
Sleeve
Blindstitch.
Quilt back

Smooth Hanging

When you pin the bottom folded edge of the sleeve to the back of the quilt, roll the edge up ¼". This adds a little extra room for the hanging rod and will help the front of the quilt hang smoothly.

BINDING

Binding adds the finishing touch to your quilt. Use your border fabric or use an accent fabric that frames your design.

Making Straight-Grain Binding

1. Use a rotary-cutter, mat, and ruler to cut two strips 2" x 42".

2. Sew the two strips together using a diagonal seam to create one long strip of binding. To make a diagonal seam, cross and pin the two strip ends at right angles with right sides together. Lay these on a flat surface and imagine the strips as a large letter *A*. Draw a line across the crossed pieces to cross the *A*, then sew along the line. Your seam will be exact, and you can unfold a continuous strip.

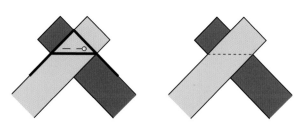

3. Trim the excess fabric, leaving a ¼"-wide seam allowance. Press the seam open to distribute the thickness of the seam.

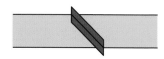

4. Fold the binding strip in half lengthwise, wrong sides together, and press with a hot steam iron.

Applying Binding

1. Machine baste with an ⅛" seam around the edge of the quilt to securely hold the three layers together. Trim any excess threads, batting, or backing even with the front of the quilt.

2. Starting in the center on a long side, align the raw edges of the binding with the raw edges of the quilt. Start sewing 3" from the end of the binding, using a ¼" seam allowance.

3. To miter the corners of the binding, stop stitching ¼" from the corner and backstitch.

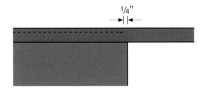

4. Fold the binding diagonally so that it extends straight up from the second edge of the quilt as shown.

5. Fold the binding down even with the second edge of the quilt and pin in place. The fold should be even with the first edge. Start sewing the binding ¼" from the fold, making sure to backstitch. Repeat for the remaining corners. End the stitching about 4" before the starting point.

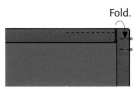

Fold.

6. To connect the ends of the binding, allow the end to overlap the beginning by 2". Unfold the binding strip and cut the end diagonally, with the shortest end of the diagonal on top, nearest to you. Turn the diagonal edge under ¼" and insert the beginning tail inside the diagonal fold. Continue sewing the binding onto the quilt.

Turn under ¼" on diagonal end.

Tuck end inside.

7. Fold the binding over the edge of the quilt so it covers the stitching on the back of the quilt. As you fold the corner to the back of the quilt, a folded miter will appear on the front.

On the back, fold one side first, and then the other, to create a mitered corner on the back.

8. Hand stitch the binding to the back of the quilt, using the traditional appliqué stitch. Hand stitch the diagonal folds at the corners.

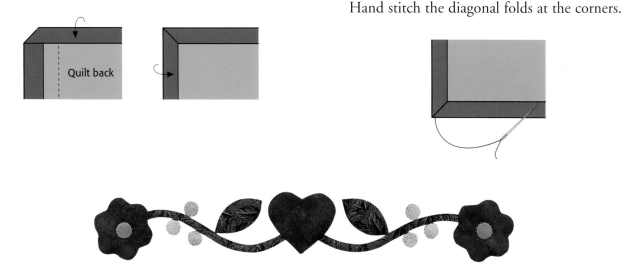

A LABEL FOR YOUR QUILT

You have made a very special quilt. Make a label for the back of it that includes the name of the quilt, your name, and the date. You may also include information about your quilt, a dedication, or a story about your quilt. Design your own label or trace the one below onto fabric. Add your lettering with a permanent marker or embroidery stitches and attach the label to your quilt with the traditional appliqué stitch.

Appliqué

Sampler

by

Mimi Dietrich

2004

Pattern Primer

THERE'S AN EASY appliqué sampler for everyone and every occasion! Choose from 20 center designs and three border treatments. Each pattern has suggested techniques for preparing and stitching the appliqués, but of course you can use your favorite methods. You can even mix techniques and design your own personal sampler. The finished size of each sampler is 16½" x 19½".

MATERIALS

Use the following yardage requirements as a general guideline when planning your quilt and purchasing fabrics. Yardage is based on 42"-wide fabric.

- ⅜ yard of background fabric for center block (⅝ yard if center block and outer borders are the same fabric)
- ⅜ yard of inspiration fabric for outer borders (⅝ yard if you cut borders on the lengthwise grain)
- ⅛ yard of accent print for inner borders
- Assorted scraps of print or solid fabrics for appliqués and border vines
- ⅝ yard of fabric for backing and sleeve
- ¼ yard of accent print for binding
- 21" x 24" piece of lightweight batting
- Buttons, embellishments, and embroidery thread as needed

CUTTING DIRECTIONS

All measurements include ¼"-wide seam allowances.

From the background fabric, cut:
- 1 center rectangle, 10½" x 13½"

From the appliqué scraps, cut:
- Pieces for your project using the appropriate pattern for your sampler

From the inner border fabric, cut:
- 2 strips, 1" x 42"; crosscut into:
  - 2 strips, 1" x 10½"
  - 2 strips, 1" x 12½"

From the outer border fabric, cut:
- 2 strips, 3½" x 42"; crosscut into:
  - 2 strips, 3½" x 13½" (cut on the lengthwise grain if you're using a directional print)
  - 2 strips, 3½" x 16½"

From the binding fabric, cut:
- 2 strips, 2" x 42"

From the backing and sleeve fabric, cut:
- 1 rectangle, 20½" x 23½"
- 1 rectangle, 6½" x 16½"

MAKING THE 9" X 12" CENTER PATTERN

The sampler center designs are printed at full size on the following pages. To make placement easier on the 9" x 12" background, make a complete center pattern referring to the following steps.

1. Cut a piece of graph paper 9" x 12". If necessary, tape two pieces of 8½" x 11" paper together horizontally and then cut them to size.

2. Draw a horizontal line 3" from the top of the paper to divide the paper into two areas: a 9" square for the appliqué design and a 3" x 9" rectangle for the letters.

3. Mark the center of the square and rectangle as shown.

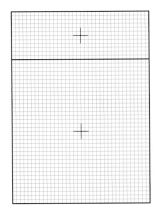

4. Choose the desired appliqué design and trace it onto the 9" square, matching the center marks.

5. Trace the corresponding letters onto the rectangle, matching the alignment marks. You can also photocopy the designs and glue them in place using a glue stick, matching the center marks.

APPLIQUÉING THE CENTER

1. Use the pattern you just made to trace the sampler design onto your center background fabric (or make a pattern overlay).

2. Appliqué the center design using your favorite technique or the pattern's suggested techniques. Mix and match appliqué techniques to sample new or different methods.

3. Appliqué the letters, using your favorite appliqué technique or the pattern's suggested techniques. Use hand or machine techniques or simply fuse the letters in place.

Lettering Tips

To keep appliquéd letters in a straight line, draw a straight line with a removable-ink marker, baste a thread line, or use a piece of masking tape to mark the base of the letters. The stitch-marked technique on page 18 will also keep the letters straight. Where applicable, embellish the letters on your sampler using two strands of embroidery floss and the chain stitch or stem stitch.

4. Keeping the design centered, trim the center rectangle to 9½" x 12½" before you sew the borders to your quilt.

ASSEMBLING YOUR SAMPLER

1. Sew the 1" x 12½" inner borders to opposite sides of the trimmed center block. Sew the 1" x 10½" inner borders to the top and bottom of the quilt. Press all seams toward the borders.

2. Sew the 3½" x 13½" outer borders to opposite sides of the quilt. Sew the 3½" x 16½" outer borders to the top and bottom of the quilt. Press all seams toward the inner borders. This makes it easy to quilt on either side of the inner borders.

BORDER DESIGNS

You have three choices for the outer borders of your sampler.

1. Let the perfect fabric inspire you! Use the inspiration fabric that accents the appliqué design for the outer border, as described above. It's fun, fast, and very easy.

2. Choose an appliquéd border. Sew 3½"-wide background-fabric borders to the sampler center. Photocopy or trace one of the border patterns on pages 94–95 and use a light box to trace the design onto the border fabric. Choose flowers or stars for the corners, and appliquéd circles or buttons for the berries. Appliqué the border vines, leaves, flowers, hearts or stars, and berries.

3. Appliqué the border corners only. Sew 3½"-wide background-fabric borders to the sampler center. Photocopy or trace the border corner pattern on page 93 and use a light box to trace the design onto the border corner. Position the designs in the upper left and lower right corners, matching the dark solid lines to the outside seam of the inner border. Appliqué the stems, leaves, heart, flower, berries, and buds.

FINISHING YOUR SAMPLER

Refer to pages 43–48 for details about quilting and finishing your easy appliqué sampler.

Designed by Mimi Dietrich; appliquéd by Annette Dietrich; machine quilted by Elaine Loughlin.

MAKING THE "ABC" SAMPLER

Refer to "Pattern Primer" on page 49 for materials requirements and assembly directions. Appliqué the pieces in alphabetical order, referring to the following hints.

Center design: Appliqué the apple using freezer paper underneath the fabric. When you remove the freezer paper from behind the apple, lightly stuff the apple with Poly-fil.

Letters: Fuse the letters to the background fabric. Outline the letters using machine buttonhole stitches and black thread.

Border: Use a fabric printed with school supplies and the alphabet to accent the appliquéd design.

Quilting: Machine quilt around the appliqués, inner border, and large printed images in the border.

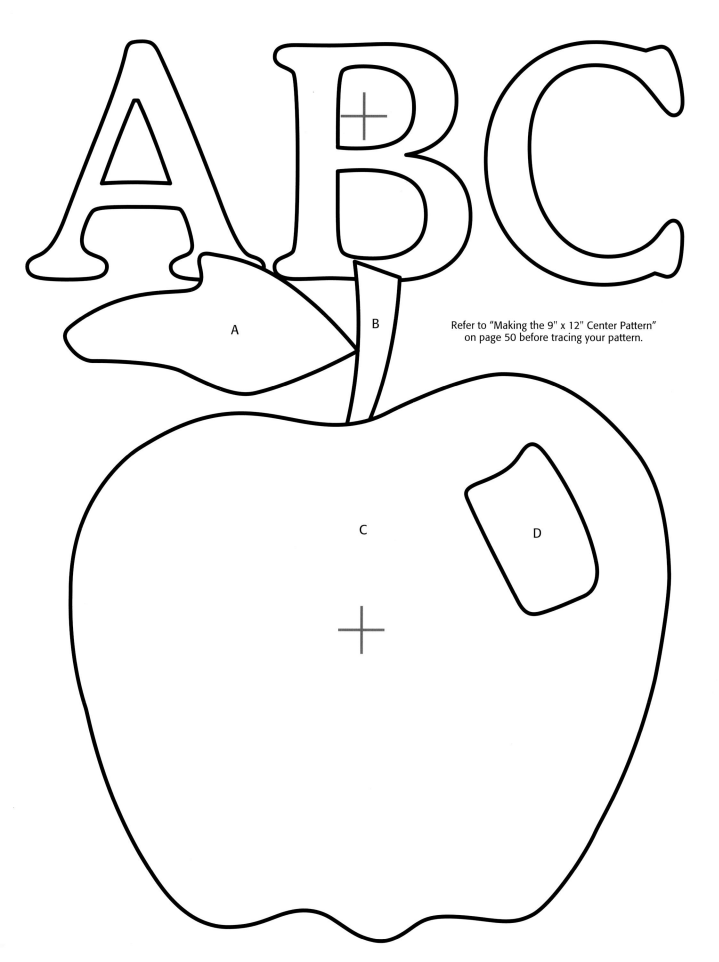

Refer to "Making the 9" x 12" Center Pattern"
on page 50 before tracing your pattern.

Designed by Mimi Dietrich; appliquéd and quilted by Genie Corbin and Vera Hall.

MAKING THE "BABY" SAMPLER

Refer to "Pattern Primer" on page 49 for materials requirements and assembly directions. Appliqué the pieces in alphabetical order, referring to the following hints.

Center Design: Appliqué the baby carriage using freezer paper underneath the fabric. Cut a 1⅛" x 12" fabric strip to make the ruched trim on the carriage. See page 35 to gather the strip and appliqué it to the carriage. See page 34 to make two yo-yos for the wheels. Sew buttons to the centers of the wheels.

Embroider the handle using the stem stitch and two strands of blue embroidery floss.

Letters: Appliqué the letters using the stitch-marked appliqué preparation technique on page 18.

Border: Referring to the pattern on page 94, appliqué the border vines, flowers, hearts, and leaves. Sew buttons to the border vine after quilting.

Quilting: Hand quilt around the appliqués and the inner border. Quilt a diagonal grid in the center background. Quilt straight lines along the border.

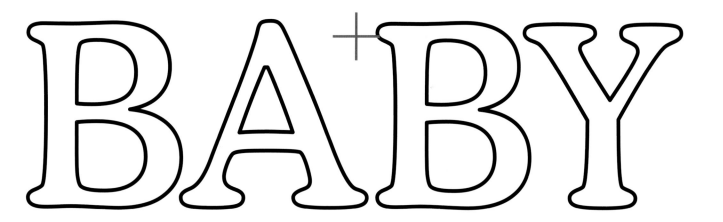

Refer to "Making the 9" x 12" Center Pattern" on page 50 before tracing your pattern.

Embroidery

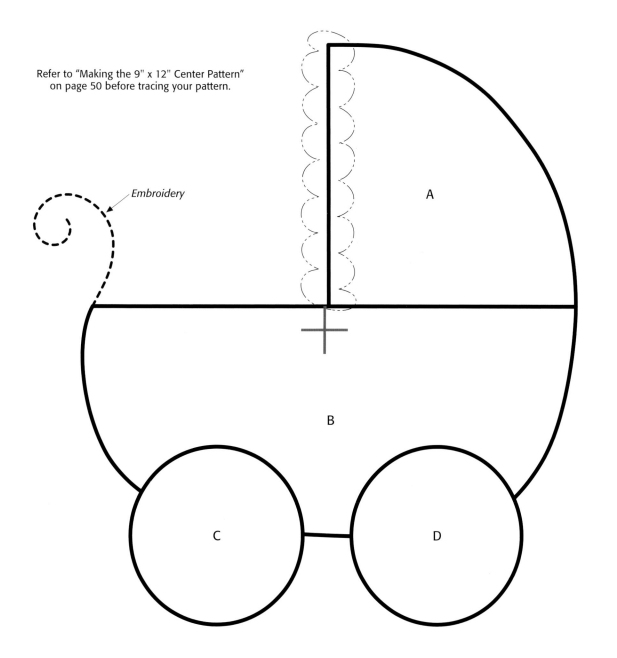

A

B

C

D

Designed, appliquéd, and quilted by Mimi Dietrich.

MAKING THE "BELIEVE" SAMPLER

Refer to "Pattern Primer" on page 49 for materials requirements and assembly directions. Appliqué the pieces in alphabetical order, referring to the following hints. This project requires an additional 4"-diameter scalloped doily.

Center design: Appliqué a 4"-diameter scalloped doily in the wing area and trim the part of the doily that extends under the angel's dress. Appliqué the angel using freezer paper underneath the fabric. Make a dimensional hanky using the folded bud technique on page 34. Outline the appliqués using the button-hole stitch and two strands of dark blue embroidery floss. Embroider the swirls using the chain stitch and two strands of ecru embroidery floss. Cut a 1⅛" x 12" strip of fabric to make the ruched angel hair. See page 35 to gather the strip and appliqué it to the angel's head. Sew two black beads to the angel's face for eyes. Add the button embellishments after you quilt your sampler.

Letters: Embroider the letters using the chain stitch and two strands of dark blue embroidery floss.

Border: Referring to the pattern on page 95, appliqué the border vine, stars, hearts, and leaves. Sew buttons to the border vine after quilting.

Quilting: Hand quilt around the appliqués and the inner border. Quilt stars in the center background.

Believe

E

F

A

D

B

C

G

H

I

Embroidery

Refer to "Making the 9" x 12" Center Pattern"
on page 50 before tracing your pattern.

Designed and quilted by Mimi Dietrich; appliquéd by Clara Murphy and Alice White.

MAKING THE "BLOOM" SAMPLER

Refer to "Pattern Primer" on page 49 for materials requirements and assembly directions. This project requires an additional strip of green fabric, 3½" x 10½", for the grass. Appliqué the pieces in alphabetical order, referring to the following hints.

Center design: To piece the background, cut a 10½" x 10½" square of background fabric and a 3½" x 10½" strip of green fabric for the grass.

Sew the grass to the bottom edge of the background. Cut the fence appliqué pieces out of lightweight fusible interfacing. Refer to page 19 to use the interfacing underneath the fabric to line the white fabric and appliqué the fence. Appliqué the leaves using freezer paper underneath the green fabric. Embroider the stems using the stem stitch and two strands of embroidery floss. Referring to page 34, make 23 gathered blossoms and attach them after you quilt your sampler.

Letters: Fuse the letters to the background fabric.

Border: Use a fabric printed with flowers to accent the appliquéd design.

Quilting: Machine quilt around the fence and inner border, then attach the dimensional flowers. Add a ladybug button for fun.

BLOOM

Refer to "Making the 9" x 12" Center Pattern" on page 50 before tracing your pattern.

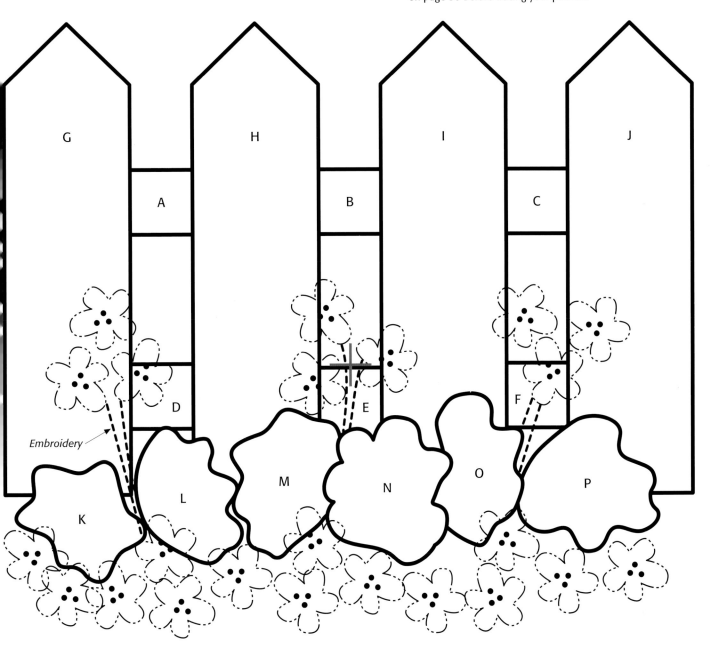

Embroidery

Designed by Mimi Dietrich; appliquéd and quilted by Kelly Kout and Bonnie Maneer.

MAKING THE "FALL" SAMPLER

Refer to "Pattern Primer" on page 49 for materials requirements and assembly directions. Appliqué the pieces in alphabetical order, referring to the following hints.

Center design: Appliqué the thin stems using stem method one on page 30. Appliqué the leaves and acorns using your favorite method.

Letters: Appliqué the letters using the stitch-marked appliqué preparation technique on page 18.

Border: Use a fabric printed with autumn leaves to accent the appliquéd design.

Quilting: Hand quilt around the appliqués and the inner border. Quilt a diagonal grid in the center background. Quilt veins in the appliquéd leaves.

Refer to "Making the 9" x 12" Center Pattern"
on page 50 before tracing your pattern.

Designed, appliquéd, and quilted by Mimi Dietrich.

MAKING THE "FAMILY" SAMPLER

Refer to "Pattern Primer" on page 49 for materials requirements and assembly directions. Appliqué the pieces in alphabetical order, referring to the following hints.

Center design: Use the stitch-marked appliqué preparation technique on page 18 to position the tree, hearts, and leaves perfectly. Needle turn the edges to appliqué. If your heart fabric will show clearly when placed on the tree fabric, simply appliqué the heart on top of the tree.

If the heart will not show clearly on the tree fabric or if you prefer the heart to appear outlined as in the photo, follow this additional step. Trace the large heart onto template plastic and cut it out. Trace the heart onto the tree trunk. Position the small heart template inside the traced large heart and trace. Cut out the small heart on the drawn line. Turn the seam allowance of the large heart to the *inside* of the drawn line, clipping seam allowances as needed. Appliqué the folded edges of the large heart to the background fabric. Position the small fabric heart inside the large heart and appliqué to the background fabric.

Letters: Embroider the letters using the chain stitch and two strands of rust embroidery floss.

Quilting: Hand quilt around the appliqués and the inner border. Quilt straight lines and clouds in the center background.

Refer to "Making the 9" x 12" Center Pattern"
on page 50 before tracing your pattern.

C

B

A

Designed by Mimi Dietrich; appliquéd and quilted by Jean Harmon and Barbara Kopf.

MAKING THE "FRIENDS" SAMPLER

Refer to "Pattern Primer" on page 49 for materials requirements and assembly directions. Appliqué the pieces in alphabetical order, referring to the following hints.

Center design: For a personal touch, trace your own hand to make the appliqué pattern. Appliqué the hand using freezer paper on top of the fabric. Use a pattern overlay or paper window to position the heart in the center of the hand. If you use a plaid fabric, trace and cut the hand and heart patterns on the bias of the fabric.

Letters: Embroider the letters using the stem stitch and two strands of blue embroidery floss.

Border: Referring to the pattern on page 95 and stem method three on page 31, appliqué the border vines using ¼" bias bars. Appliqué the hearts, leaves, and berries using the stitch-marked appliqué preparation technique on page 18. Fuse the stars in the corners and outline with a buttonhole stitch.

Quilting: Hand quilt around the appliqués and the inner border. Quilt a diagonal grid in the center background. Quilt straight lines along the border.

A

B

Refer to "Making the 9" x 12" Center Pattern"
on page 50 before tracing your pattern.

Designed, appliquéd, and quilted by Mimi Dietrich.

MAKING THE "HOME" SAMPLER

NOTE: *To make a quilt similar to the one shown on this book's cover, simply substitute the "ABC" patterns on page 53 for the "Home" lettering shown on the facing page.*

Refer to "Pattern Primer" on page 49 for materials requirements and assembly directions. Appliqué the pieces in alphabetical order, referring to the following hints.

Center design: To piece the background, cut an 11½" x 10½" rectangle of background fabric. Appliqué the house and door. Cut a 2½" x 10½" strip of green fabric for the grass. Sew the grass to the bottom edge of the background. Appliqué the flower stems using stem method two on page 30. Appliqué the house roof, star, bird, and flowers using freezer paper underneath the fabric. Use a pattern overlay or paper window to position the heart on the house. Add black beads for the doorknob and bird's eye.

Letters: Appliqué the letters using the stitch-marked appliqué preparation technique on page 18.

Border: Referring to the pattern on page 94, appliqué the border vines using stem method two on page 30. Appliqué the hearts, flowers, leaves, and berries.

Quilting: Hand quilt around the appliqués and the inner border. Quilt a diagonal grid in the center background. Quilt straight lines along the border.

Bead placement

HOME

F

H

G

C

D

E

P

Q

J

K   L

A

B

Bead placement

I

M   N

O

R   S

Refer to "Making the 9" x 12" Center Pattern"
on page 50 before tracing your pattern.

Designed by Mimi Dietrich; appliquéd and quilted by Dori Mayer and Angie Dukehart.

MAKING THE "LOVE" SAMPLER

Refer to "Pattern Primer" on page 49 for materials requirements and assembly directions. Appliqué the pieces in alphabetical order, referring to the following hints.

Center design: Fuse the wavy-edged square to the background fabric. Use a pattern overlay or paper window to position the two hearts in the center. Create the look of a doily by outlining the square with buttonhole stitch using two strands of pink embroidery floss. Add buttons after you quilt your sampler.

Letters: Fuse the letters to the background fabric.

Border: Referring to the pattern on page 93, appliqué the border corner vines, flower, heart, leaves, and berries. Make dimensional folded buds using the technique on page 34.

Quilting: Machine quilt around the appliqués and the inner border. Hand quilt around the border appliqués. Quilt straight lines along the border.

Button placement

C

B

A

Refer to "Making the 9" x 12" Center Pattern"
on page 50 before tracing your pattern.

Designed by Mimi Dietrich; appliquéd and quilted by Anita Askins.

Making the "Mom" Sampler

Refer to "Pattern Primer" on page 49 for materials requirements and assembly directions. Appliqué the pieces in alphabetical order, referring to the following hints.

Center design: Appliqué the thin stems using stem method one on page 30. Appliqué the flowers and leaves using freezer paper underneath the fabric. Make dimensional folded buds with the technique on page 34.

Letters: Appliqué the letters using the stitch-marked appliqué preparation technique on page 18.

Border: Referring to the pattern on page 93, appliqué the border corner vines, flower, heart, leaves, and berries. Make dimensional folded buds with the technique on page 34.

Quilting: Hand quilt around the appliqués and the inner border. Quilt a diagonal grid in the center background. Quilt parallel lines ¾" apart on the borders.

Refer to "Making the 9" x 12" Center Pattern" on page 50 before tracing your pattern.

Designed by Mimi Dietrich; appliquéd by Mary Stewart and Connie Waxter; machine quilted by Pamela Budesheim.

MAKING THE "PEACE" SAMPLER

Refer to "Pattern Primer" on page 49 for materials requirements and assembly directions. Appliqué the pieces in alphabetical order, referring to the following hints.

Center design: Cut the dove appliqué pieces out of lightweight fusible interfacing. Referring to page 19, use the interfacing to line the white fabric and appliqué the doves. Use a pattern overlay or paper window to position the hearts on top of the doves.

Letters: Embroider the letters using the chain stitch and two strands of white embroidery floss.

Border: Referring to the pattern on page 95, appliqué the border, cutting appliqué pieces from the multicolored background fabric. Make perfect circles using thin metal washers as templates.

Quilting: Machine quilt around the appliqués, the embroidery stitches, and the inner border. Quilt clouds in the background fabric and meander in the border background.

Peace

Quilting

Refer to "Making the 9" x 12" Center Pattern"
on page 50 before tracing your pattern.

Designed by Mimi Dietrich; appliquéd by Debra McCarriar; quilted by Diana Harper.

MAKING THE "SEW" SAMPLER

Refer to "Pattern Primer" on page 49 for materials requirements and assembly directions. Appliqué the pieces in alphabetical order, referring to the following hints.

Center design: Appliqué the sewing machine, spool of thread, and pincushion using freezer paper underneath the fabric. Add details (pins, needle, and strawberry stem) using stem stitches and two strands of embroidery floss. Add buttons for machine dials and pin heads after you quilt your sampler.

Letters: Fuse the letters to the background fabric. Outline the letters using machine buttonhole stitches and matching thread.

Border: Use a fabric printed with sewing supplies to accent the appliquéd design.

Quilting: Hand quilt around the appliqués and the inner border. Quilt a diagonal grid in the center background. Quilt straight lines along the border, following the printed fabric.

Refer to "Making the 9" x 12" Center Pattern"
on page 50 before tracing your pattern.

Button placement

Embroidery

Designed by Mimi Dietrich; appliquéd and quilted by Betty Morton.

MAKING THE "SNOW" SAMPLER

Refer to "Pattern Primer" on page 49 for materials requirements and assembly directions. Appliqué the pieces in alphabetical order, referring to the following hints.

Center design: Iron lightweight fusible interfacing to the wrong side of the white snowflake fabric. This lines the white fabric so the background fabric will not shadow through it. Fuse the lined snowflake to the background fabric. Fuse the hearts in place. Outline the designs using matching thread and machine satin stitches.

Letters: Iron lightweight fusible interfacing to the wrong side of the white letter fabric. Fuse the lined letters to the background fabric. Outline the letters using matching thread and machine satin stitches.

Border: Use a dark fabric printed with snowflakes to accent the appliquéd design.

Quilting: Machine quilt around the appliqués and the inner border.

Refer to "Making the 9" x 12" Center Pattern"
on page 50 before tracing your pattern.

Designed by Mimi Dietrich; appliquéd by Kay Worley; quilted by Norma Campbell.

MAKING THE "SUN" SAMPLER

Refer to "Pattern Primer" on page 49 for materials requirements and assembly directions. Appliqué the pieces in alphabetical order, referring to the following hints.

Center design: Appliqué the sun's rays and face using freezer paper underneath the fabric. Refer to page 32 to appliqué the circles using heavy paper. Fuse the cheeks to the face and sew two black beads to the face for eyes. Embroider the mouth and eyebrows using the stem stitch and two strands of black embroidery floss.

Letters: Fuse the letters to the background fabric.

Border: Use a fabric printed with suns to accent the appliquéd design.

Quilting: Hand quilt around the appliqués and the inner border. Quilt rays in the center background fabric. Quilt straight lines along the border.

Refer to "Making the 9" x 12" Center Pattern"
on page 50 before tracing your pattern.

Designed by Mimi Dietrich; appliquéd by Nancy Egan; quilted by Julie Bradley.

MAKING THE "TEA" SAMPLER

Refer to "Pattern Primer" on page 49 for materials requirements and assembly directions. Appliqué the pieces in alphabetical order, referring to the following hints.

Center design: Appliqué the teapot using freezer paper underneath the fabric. Use a pattern overlay or paper window to position the heart in the center of the pot. Outline the teapot and its lid using hand buttonhole stitches and two strands of red embroidery floss.

Letters: Fuse the letters to the background fabric. Outline the letters using hand buttonhole stitches and two strands of matching embroidery floss.

Border: Use a fabric printed with teacups to accent the appliquéd design.

Quilting: Hand quilt around the appliqués and the inner border.

Refer to "Making the 9" x 12" Center Pattern" on page 50 before tracing your pattern.

Embroidery

A

B

Designed by Mimi Dietrich; appliquéd by Barbara Bennett; quilted by Barbara Laskowski.

MAKING THE "THANKS" SAMPLER

Refer to "Pattern Primer" on page 49 for materials requirements and assembly directions. Appliqué the pieces in alphabetical order, referring to the following hints.

Center design: Use a basket-weave print for the basket and bias-cut handle. Fuse the appliqué pieces to the background fabric using a pattern overlay for placement. Outline the appliqués using buttonhole stitches and two strands of matching embroidery floss.

Letters: Embroider the letters using the chain stitch and two strands of blue embroidery floss.

Border: Use a fabric printed with baskets to accent the appliquéd design.

Quilting: Hand quilt around the appliqués and the inner border. Quilt a diagonal grid in the center background. Quilt straight lines along the border.

Refer to "Making the 9" x 12" Center Pattern" on page 50 before tracing your pattern.

Designed by Mimi Dietrich; appliquéd by the staff at Seminole Sampler quilt shop; quilted by Libbie Rollman.

MAKING THE "USA" SAMPLER

Refer to "Pattern Primer" on page 49 for materials requirements and assembly directions. This project requires additional strips of red and blue fabric for the pieced background. Appliqué the pieces in alphabetical order, referring to the following hints.

Center design: *Please note that the dimensions given for piecing are exact and do not allow for trimming after completing the appliqué.* To piece the background, cut a 4½" x 9½" rectangle of off-white background fabric for the top "USA" area. Cut a 3½" x 9½" rectangle of blue for the center star area. Cut four 1½" x 5½" strips from red fabric. Cut five 1½" x 5½" strips from the off-white fabric. Sew these strips together to make the striped area.

Refer to the photo to piece the background fabric. Appliqué the stars using freezer paper on top of the gold fabric.

Letters: Appliqué the letters using the stitch-marked appliqué preparation technique on page 18.

Border: Referring to the pattern on page 95, appliqué the border vines, stars, hearts, leaves, and berries.

Quilting: Hand quilt around the appliqués, stripes, and the inner border. Quilt diagonal lines on the border. Sew blue star buttons on the gold stars after the quilting is completed.

Refer to "Making the 9" x 12" Center Pattern"
on page 50 before tracing your pattern.

Designed by Mimi Dietrich; appliquéd by Polly Mello; quilted by Kathy Siuta.

MAKING THE "WELCOME" SAMPLER

Refer to "Pattern Primer" on page 49 for materials requirements and assembly directions. Appliqué the pieces in alphabetical order, referring to the following hints.

Center design: Use the stitch-marked appliqué preparation technique on page 18 to position the pineapples and leaves perfectly. Needle turn the edges to appliqué the pieces to the background.

Letters: Embroider the letters using the chain stitch and two strands of green embroidery floss.

Border: Referring to the pattern on page 94, appliqué the border vines, flowers, hearts, leaves, and berries.

Quilting: Hand quilt around the appliqués and the inner border. Quilt texture lines in the pineapples. Quilt a diagonal grid in the center background. Quilt straight lines along the border.

Refer to "Making the 9" x 12" Center Pattern"
on page 50 before tracing your pattern.

C

A

B

Designed by Mimi Dietrich; appliquéd by Lynn Irwin; quilted by Fran Timmins.

MAKING THE "WISH" SAMPLER

Refer to "Pattern Primer" on page 49 for materials requirements and assembly directions. Appliqué the pieces in alphabetical order, referring to the following hints.

Center design: Appliqué the candles, cake, and plate using freezer paper underneath the fabric. Outline the white cake using a hand stem stitch and two strands of pink embroidery floss. Cut two strips, 1⅛" x 26" and

1⅛" x 28", to make the ruched icing. See page 35 to gather the strips and appliqué them to the cake.

Letters: Appliqué the letters using the stitch-marked appliqué preparation technique on page 18.

Border: Use a fabric printed with balloons to accent the appliquéd design.

Quilting: Hand quilt around the appliqués and the inner border. Quilt a diagonal grid in the center background. Quilt straight lines along the border.

Refer to "Making the 9" x 12" Center Pattern"
on page 50 before tracing your pattern.

Designed by Mimi Dietrich; appliquéd and quilted by Ann Christy and Penny Seymore.

MAKING THE "QUILT" SAMPLER

Refer to "Pattern Primer" on page 49 for materials requirements and assembly directions. This project requires additional fabric for the pieced background.

CUTTING FOR THE CENTER

From tan background print, cut:
- 1 rectangle, 3½" x 10½"
- 4 rectangles, 3½" x 4½"
- 4 squares, 3½" x 3½"

From the blue print, cut:
- 8 squares, 2½" x 2½"

From the dark tan center print, cut:
- 1 square, 4½" x 4½"

CENTER ASSEMBLY

1. Using a pencil, draw a diagonal line on the wrong side of each blue print square.

2. With right sides together, place a blue square in a corner of a tan 3½" x 4½" rectangle as shown.

3. Sew on the line and trim away the excess fabric leaving a ¼" seam allowance. Press the seam toward the blue triangle.

4. Place a blue square in the adjacent corner as shown. Sew, trim, and press as in step 3. Repeat to make four units.

Make 4.

5. Sew two pieced units to opposite sides of the 4½" dark tan square. Press toward the dark tan square.

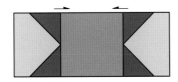

6. Sew a tan 3½" square to opposite ends of the remaining units from step 4 as shown. Press seams toward the tan squares. Make two.

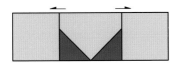

Make 2.

7. Sew the units together to make an Evening Star block. Press.

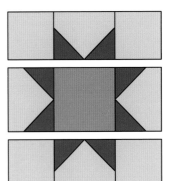

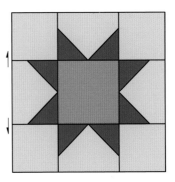

8. Use a pattern overlay or paper window to position the heart in the center of the Evening Star block. Appliqué the heart in place.

9. Sew the 3½" x 10½" tan rectangle to the top of the star block.

10. Trim the center to 9½" x 12½".

SAMPLER COMPLETION

Appliqué the pieces in alphabetical order, referring to the following hints.

Letters: Fuse the letters to the top background rectangle.

Border: Referring to the pattern on page 94, appliqué the border vines, flowers, hearts, leaves, and berries. Add buttons after you quilt your sampler.

Quilting: Hand quilt around the appliqués and the inner border. Quilt ¼" around the star.

A

CORNER BORDER PATTERN

Corner Border Pattern A
Upper Left

See "Border Designs" on page 51 in the Pattern Primer.

Corner Border Pattern B
Lower Right

E

I (½")

A

J

K

C

G

Center

F (½")

B

L

M

N

D

O

P

Q

H

Side center

Center
heart
G/H

See "Border Designs"
on page 51 in the
Pattern Primer.

Border Pattern A
Upper Left
Lower Right

Border Pattern B
Upper Right
Lower Left

I (½")

Center

Side center

About the Author

MIMI DIETRICH has been appliquéing for as long as she can remember! Her first quilt, made for her son in 1974, was a Sunbonnet Sue–Overall Bill quilt with a dimensional hankie in Bill's pocket. Mimi has lived in Baltimore all of her life and is inspired by the beautiful Baltimore Album appliqué quilts made in her city 150 years ago. She teaches appliqué classes all over the United States. In *Easy Appliqué Samplers,* she designed bright little wall quilts using easy appliqué designs and a sampler of the many appliqué techniques she enjoys. Her students in her "Graduate" appliqué class stitched many of the samplers for this book. She hopes that these colorful projects will inspire new stitchers to love appliqué as much as she does!